Animal Spirit Guides

An Easy to Follow Guide on Discovering and Harnessing Your Power Animal

(Unleashing the Power of Shamanism, Animal Spirit Guides, Shamanic Totems, Power Animals)

Debra Gonyea

Published By **Darby Connor**

Debra Gonyea

All Rights Reserved

Animal Spirit Guides: An Easy to Follow Guide on Discovering and Harnessing Your Power Animal (Unleashing the Power of Shamanism, Animal Spirit Guides, Shamanic Totems, Power Animals)

ISBN 978-0-9958659-1-4

No part of this guidebook shall be reproduced in any form without permission in writing from the publisher except in the case of brief quotations embodied in critical articles or reviews.

Legal & Disclaimer

The information contained in this ebook is not designed to replace or take the place of any form of medicine or professional medical advice. The information in this ebook has been provided for educational & entertainment purposes only.

The information contained in this book has been compiled from sources deemed reliable, and it is accurate to the best of the Author's knowledge; however, the Author cannot guarantee its accuracy and validity and cannot be held liable for any errors or omissions. Changes are periodically made to this book. You must consult your doctor or get professional medical advice before using any of the suggested remedies, techniques, or information in this book.

Upon using the information contained in this book, you agree to hold harmless the Author from and against any damages, costs, and expenses, including any legal fees potentially resulting from the application of any of the information provided by this guide. This disclaimer applies to any damages or injury caused by the use and application, whether directly or indirectly, of any advice or information presented, whether for breach of contract, tort, negligence, personal injury, criminal intent, or under any other cause of action.

You agree to accept all risks of using the information presented inside this book. You need to consult a professional medical practitioner in order to ensure you are both able and healthy enough to participate in this program.

TABLE OF CONTENTS

Chapter 1: Significance & Types Of Spirit Animal Guide 1

Chapter 2: Spirit Animal, According To Your Zodiac Sign...................................... 54

Chapter 3: How To Talk At The Facet Of Your Parent Spirit Animal....................... 74

Chapter 4: How To Discover Your Spirit Animals 102

Chapter 5: What Are Spirit Guides? 116

Chapter 6: Spirit Animals – What Are They? 168

Chapter 7: Tips On How To Find Your Spirit Animal 181

Chapter 1: Significance & Types Of Spirit Animal Guide

You should come across severa animal spirit guides, however the ones are the maximum commonplace ones:

Lifelong

This is the animal spirit guide you may have for the relaxation of your existence. It can also need to show as an entire lot as you at any element to your life, but once it does, it could no longer leave till the give up of your days. It's viable that you have a completely unique bond with this animal or that it has appeared to you previously. It's feasible that you've mentioned this monster for lots lifetimes.

Journey

Journey: It serves as a road map to keep you at the proper path. When you need their help at unique instances in your existence, those creatures can arrive rapid and leave surely as . They should linger for most effective a second or for plenty months. These usually come while a journey is prepared to start and stay with you until that particular life occasion is over.

Message

It can appear in the future as a "wait a minute" second to provide you with a warning to a trouble. Consider the animal's message to you and be privy to it.

Shadow

Shadow: When you get over your fear of this animal, it turns into taken into consideration certainly one of your best property. This spirit animal represents the aspect of your self in which you lack the most self-guarantee or the difficulty of your self that you find the least attractive.

Purpose

This animal spirit manual will seem for specific occasions, rites, or journeys. My wild boar animal spirit manual may not go together with me to the underworld, so the Black Panther suggests as an awful lot as experience with me as an opportunity. This great takes place as quickly as I'm hedge the usage of (touring) to the underworld. My frog spirit manual behaves further; he only joins me after I am drumming.

Animal Medicine

We can begin to see glimpses of each animal's treatment through searching animals of their herbal habitats and watching the behaviors that go with them. This statistics therefore allows us to honor the animal spirit, connect with it, and use its magic in our day by day lifestyles and spell paintings.

Spirit animal's medication can gain us in some of strategies.

* It can provide you the fortitude, energy, and ardour to overcome boundaries or hurdles to your life.

* It may additionally assist you apprehend a essential choice you could want to make.

*It can provide tips for a particular project and turn out to be privy to solutions to ambiguous problems.

* Tapping into your inner sources is probably beneficial.

* Overcoming your problems may be made less complicated.

* It can result in your real traits and untapped capability.

* It can increase your body's resistance in competition to sickness.

*When you are unwell, it could enhance your recovery.

* In unique times, it can assist you in studying important information.

* It can beneficial useful resource in getting better out of vicinity devices.

* It can preserve you constant and assist you in heading off likely fatal or dangerous instances.

* It can useful resource in protective you inside the path of intellectual, emotional, or bodily suffering.

* It can offer you comfort whilst instances are tough.

* It will let you in growing closer bonds with others.

* It can resource to your improvement of self-assurance.

* It also can moreover direct your spiritual development.

Roles a spirit animals play

Messenger and Counselor

Your spirit animal can provide you alternatives that could assist with alternatives or alternatives in this capacity through supporting you in statistics troubles and offering answers and assistance. Your animal spirit guide can provide advice at the first-rate direction of motion and behaviors to adopt.

Protector

In this capacity, your spirit animal manual can provide you with the fortitude, courage, and power to deal with something that comes your manner. It also can function a warning at the same time as hazard is close by or while matters are approximately to move unpleasant. Each animal will respond to situations in a unique manner, consequently it's far vital to pay close to interest to what they may be attempting to inform you. Different animals will reply to hazard in remarkable strategies.

Teacher

Your animal spirit animal may be a brilliant instructor that teaches you a manner to make the most of your internal spirit and energy all through your existence. The animals that often display up can supply important data, and they'll maintain doing so till we have understood and placed the lesson into exercise.

Healer

Excellent healers, animal spirit guides may additionally furthermore teach us on a manner to cope with every our very very own emotional, bodily, and non secular ills further to the ones of others. You will collect recuperation energy out of your animal spirit guide. Additionally, it could help hasten the recuperation way through demonstrating the top-first-rate direction of movement or technique to rent.

Guide

Your animal spirit manual will function all the aforementioned features similarly to greater ones within the course of your complete life. Your lifestyles will trade for the higher and you will wonder the way you ever controlled with out your guide as soon as you have located it.

Common Spirit Animals and Their Meaning

Reference the listing of spirit animals described below, and pay close to attention to any creatures you could have nowadays seen. Their meanings may additionally moreover provide belief into why they crossed your path.

Eagle

When you see an eagle eagle, it is time to get again on your spiritual course. They are right here to characteristic a reminder for us to have a look at our hearts in place of our thoughts all the time. If an eagle represents you in my opinion, it indicates that while you're lighthearted, you need to live grounded.

Eagles are symbolic of light, spirit, and healing. By mending your self, you may more actually connect to your religious direction. This ancestor's spirit animal possesses divine devices and magic attention.

Spider

It serves as a reminder as a way to layout the existence you need to stay while you spot masses of spiders on your actual lifestyles or desires. These courses are meant to tell us while to start constructing the life we want due to the truth spiders are regarded for weaving trendy webs and having staying energy even as taking snap shots their prey.

Spiders are some other photograph for the lady and the energy of lady energy. If this serves as your guide (within the meanwhile), be patient with yourself and discover your innovative aspect. Projects, jobs, and accomplishments all require time, and the magic lies inside the way in region of the final results.

Think of your self like a spider weaving a web that you need to construct for yourself. Then, wait patiently for the outcomes of your hard work to materialize.

Hummingbird

Hummingbirds are brimming with lightness, kinship, and pace. Hummingbirds are a image of connection, playfulness, and versatility for your existence. Hummingbirds be part of plant life and plant life, and no matter their diminutive length, they'll be capable of awesome achievements. They can battle and adapt to any scenario at the same time as preserving a thrilled and active persona.

Try to connect with the fun of existence and try no longer to take subjects too considerably at the identical time as a hummingbird is round, whether or not or not for a long term or quality for a day. They are proper right here to remind us to have fun and that connection, whether or now not or no longer it is with near ones or a better strength, is what subjects maximum ultimately.

Hummingbirds can encourage you and function a reminder that the entirety takes area for a purpose. Instead than trying to persuade effects, alter for your surroundings.

The Crow

The crow surely can provide quite a few magic and secrets and techniques and techniques, in spite of the reality that it could now not appear like the proper spirit guide. Crows are renowned for having a higher perspective, being adaptable, and, most significantly, having "trickster" persona kinds. If the crow has been acting to you, whether or not in goals or on the equal time as you're conscious, undergo in thoughts your dating to lifestyles and its magic.

To see the surprise in the whole thing this is occurring to you and round you, try to undertake a higher mindset and boom your stage of reputation for your life.

Crows are taken into consideration to be the favored spirit animal of those who utilize magic and have the capability to govern the universe thinking about the reality that they will be associated with existence's magic.

Butterfly

A butterfly performing for your life is seemed as one of the most iconic omens of profound exchange and transformation. It's feasible that you're going through numerous degrees of lifestyles and in reality evolving from the internal out.

There is a revel in of loss of life and rebirth right here; possibly part of your antique self is passing away so a more moderen, progressed model of you may emerge. The idea of "being mild" and floating above worldly issues is conveyed by using manner of butterflies as nicely.

Owl

One of the more unusual spirit animals is the owl. A real signal from the cosmos will come your way if an owl takes region to skip your course. The owl is a spirit animal that stands for know-how, closeness, and instinct.

When you discover this guide, you is probably going thru a transition or on the point of start a journey in that you are exploring the unknown.

The owl has the functionality to decide truth from lies. The owl possesses intuition and might apprehend topics that most human beings normally can't. You also can see beyond the delusions produced with the aid of our minds while this animal's spirit is present for you.

Hawk

The hawk stands for bravery, self-attention, reality, and attitude. Due to their superior imaginative and prescient and capacity to appearance the reality of any scenario for what it is, hawks are quite expert as spirit publications. Additionally, the hawk stands for inner guidance and instinct.

When you study a hawk, you are being cautioned that the time has come on the way to study in which you are in lifestyles and decide what to do next. To see your life from a better mindset, use the Hawk's acute eye. Then, connect with your inner consciousness and instinct and permit these things lead you.

Grasshopper

You will be required to take a soar of faith while this tiny man enters your life. Grasshoppers are innovative and seize opportunities to reinforce in lifestyles.

Grasshoppers are seen as fortunate symptoms and signs and exquisite success in state-of-the-art. They are constantly transferring and persevering with due to the fact they're conveying messages. If you keep bumping into grasshoppers, it could be a sign which you need to make a choice and flow forward with guarantee that the final effects can be excessive quality.

Bear

Since bears are the various best animals on the planet and probable the first-rate animal to North America, it makes sense that those tendencies are associated with strength and control,

Native Americans held a immoderate regard for the grizzly undergo, and those who had been believed to have bears as their spirit animals had been visible as being robust, self-confident, and ready to behave while important.

The use of the animal inside the name of Chief Standing Bear, a Ponca whose well-known involvement in a civil rights motion in 1879 is a watershed inside the records of Native American contributors of the family within the United States, serves to underline this thing.

Along with representing repose, seclusion, and quiet time, the endure furthermore corresponds to the idea of protracted hibernation.

Cat

Typically, the number one trouble that includes thoughts even as we hold in mind cats is our domesticated pets. Cute animals that spend the bulk of their time mendacity round and napping, however from time to time come over for a few hobby.

But cats are a ways extra complicated than that, and while you consider them as a spirit animal, you have to keep in mind each member of the pussycat family, in addition to tigers, cougars, lions, and leopards.

In moderate of this, cats represent a super shape of meanings. There is, of course, braveness, similarly to staying power and a readiness to attend, as a looking lion may moreover, for the right time to behave.

Additionally, there's independence, hobby, and an adventurous mindset. Cats often spend pretty some time outdoor at night time prowling and exploring on their very own. People who revel in touring and trying to find a deeper know-how in their surroundings are often those who find out cats as their spirit animals. They are out exploring and studying approximately the arena.

Snake

Snakes are but every different animal symbolically related to healing. It's exciting what number of civilizations also partner snakes with threat, that is comprehensible given the abundance of lethal species; but, some people additionally view snakes as a supply of life.

The Greek deity of recovery snakes wrapped round a rod are used to depict Aesclepius, and this photo has come to be appeared as a image for remedy. This is because of the belief that snakes are pushed through their instinctual desires and are constantly in contact with the lifestyles energy of the Earth.

If a snake represents your spirit animal, you likely have a sturdy instinctual problem and are able to draw lifestyles and strength from the herbal global.

Generally speaking, if the snake seems as your spirit animal:

Snakes are considered to be spirit animals of transformation and restoration.

The snake's spirit is associated with life strain and primordial power.

Spiritual assistance is one of the snake spirit animal's meanings.

When it includes modifications in existence, whether or not or not they are taking place on a bodily, emotional, or spiritual diploma, the snake can function a manual.

Elephant

Elephants are portrayed as symbols of power, understanding, concept, and reverence in masses of 1-of-a-type cultures. Both in mythology and facts, their may want to possibly is well-known. They continue to be associated with this strong connotation even nowadays, making them the best spirit animal for anyone who desires to take manage in their lifestyles.

Typically, the elephant stands for:

* Resilience

* Power

* Wisdom

* Gut instinct

* Survival

* Motherliness and maternal intuition

* The consistency of our lives

* Physical fortitude and imperviousness

* The ability to bear and the selection to stay an extended life

* Mother Earth

*An example of the way circus-like lifestyles is (once in a while crazy, but entire of surprise)

Elephants are recognizable animals that are broadly diagnosed for having a massive fashion of symbolic meanings. In preferred, although, the elephant represents power and majesty. This celestial animal represents durability and facts. Elephants are considered thru many people as more than surely a adorable animal; they're seemed as a source of energy and safety further to a chum who will assist them for the duration of attempting times.

Bat

The look of the bat for your lifestyles is a sign of coming close to close to transformation. He dreams you to be privy to the symptoms all round you. At first, the adjustment should seem terrifying, but you have to allow waft of the antique physical video games and techniques of thinking that now not serve your higher cause. They will absolutely impede your development.

Dolphin

The dolphin is a photograph of balance and concord. Dolphins are notably clever creatures that still have a robust connection to their instincts. Dolphins are also a example of each safety and rebirth. Their carefree attitude serves as a reminder for all and sundry to take life with a laugh and delight. Those that turn out to be aware about with the dolphin totem are usually calm and type however private a strong inner middle.

The dolphin is a complex mammal that has been associated with an entire lot of meanings in some unspecified time in the future of records, along with:

* Harmony and peace

* Security

* Laughter and playfulness

* Resurrection

* Inner fortitude

* Collaboration

Dolphins have a better intelligence to counterbalance their herbal instincts. Instead than overanalyzing situations, they agree with their gut emotions and intuition. With fantastic species, together with human beings, they coexist fortuitously. Dolphins regularly swim and play close to humans and boats. Their compassionate tendencies train us to appearance the first-rate in all people and artwork to create concord into our lives and the lives of those spherical us.

Bear

The undergo is a picture of electricity and stability within the international of spirit animals. This animal has prolonged been authentic as a sturdy totem, giving individuals who need it the fortitude to confront hassle. It is a robust spirit animal that may assist each bodily and emotional restoration while you recall that it's miles in track with the cycles of nature and the floor.

For those who've a go through as their totem animal, the following meanings will feature idea:

* The go through's symbolic this means that is within the fundamental one in every of power and self notion.

* Remaining strong in the face of problem; appearing decisively

* The bear's spirit approach that it's time to heal or to apply one's restoration powers to gain oneself or others.

* The go through medication emphasizes the fee of quiet time, repose, and solitude.

* The go through spirit gives effective grounding forces.

Dragon

The myriad myths surrounding the records of the Dragon supply it mystique and tie it all together. This bold and fascinating monster has served because of the fact the model for limitless works of literature, poetry, paintings, movie, and distinctive varieties of expression. Many cultures have a excessive regard for the dragon, that is each reputable or deeply feared.

Bee

Few animals play a feature that is as big, both truly and metaphorically, due to the fact the bee. If a bee is your spirit animal, you're privy to your particular function as a writer in both your very own existence and the lives of others. This small however formidable creature will characteristic your guide, presenting you with the muse and braveness you need to finish even the maximum tough duties. The bee has an extended data of serving as a photo for perseverance, social attention, and religious boom. We need to take use of the power and understanding that this exciting animal has to offer simply so we will have a look at plenty from it.

The symbolism of the bee incorporates a tremendous sort of collective, non-public, physical, and religious meanings:

* Effective interaction and communication

* Tenacity and perseverance

* The capacity to create and envision

* The capability to apprehend and understand completely

* Life's sweetness

* Love and generosity

* Authenticity

* The preference to take a look at oneself

* Affinity for the divine and slight

* Consonance with the natural rhythms of life

* Healing or boosted energy

* Reproduction and output

* Assistance and prodding

The bee's symbolism is a strong instance of their existence and the numerous myths that this insect has fostered all through history. Ancient legendary recollections claim that bees supply a boost to and purify the soul. They growth us to the recognition of civilization-constructing heroes with the aid of using fostering male harmony via their knowledge and the heroic deeds they perform no matter their diminutive stature.

Dear

If the deer is your spirit animal, you are pretty intuitive and touchy. Your affinities with this animal provide you the capability to triumph over difficulties with poise. You've mastered the stability among firmness and tact in your method. The functionality to stay watchful, act hastily, and bear in thoughts their instincts to get out of the most difficult conditions is some component that the deer totem understanding bestows onto the ones who've a strong connection to this animal.

The connotations of the deer mixture every gentle, touchy inclinations with tenacity and remedy:

* Mildness

* Readiness to triumph over challenges in lifestyles with grace

* Connecting with one's internal little one and innocence

* Having empathy and intuition

* Alertness and rapid course-converting talents

* The capability to renew magically, in contact with the mysteries of lifestyles

Dog

Each breed of dog has its very very personal specific developments. If a remarkable breed has entered your existence, remember the trends that set it apart due to the reality the canine is probably purported to very very own those tendencies as nicely.

Dogs are committed to every body they consider a member in their family. Numerous historic debts exist of puppies who remained with the resource in their proprietors' factors despite amazing private danger. If a canine seems for your life, it could endorse that you are a dependable and honest friend. The canine totem might also moreover display up in a person's life as a reminder that loyalty exists at the same time as they may be feeling lonely or betrayed.

These are only some of the greater commonplace ones; there are a ton extra.

Frog

As a spirit animal, the frog serves as a reminder of the fleeting essence of lifestyles. This spirit animal serves as our best friend at some point of times of change as a illustration of trade and transition. It is carefully associated with the water element and helps us understand the woman realm of feelings and energies similarly to the cleaning approach, whether or not or now not or not it's miles physical, emotional, greater religious, or lively.

Frog symbolism may be seen in numerous cultures anywhere inside the international. This animal is normally associated with the showering properties of the water element. The frog represents:

* Purifying

* Rebirth and renewal

* Abundance, fertility

* Mutation, evolution

* Mysteries of lifestyles and orthodox information

Horse

The horse is a example of character power, passion, and a preference for freedom. It is one of the spirit animals that well-knownshows a powerful motivation that includes someone through lifestyles. Whether this animal spirit guide is portrayed as wild, tamed, moving freely or restrained, the symbolism of the horse differs.

In favored, horses stand for:

* Your motivation, the element that maintains you going via lifestyles

* The harmony amongst your instinctive and tamed sides of your self is a secondary symbolism for the pony spirit animal.

* Sexual energy, in particular but now not best male electricity

* Powerful feelings and excessive wishes

A thorough evaluation of the horse spirit animal consists of every first-rate and horrific interpretations of this animal's symbolism, allowing you to select the interpretation that maximum appeals to you.

Lion

The lion is the most far sighted warrior in competition to limitations in lifestyles inside the worldwide of spirit animals. The lion is a image of bravery and electricity in overcoming challenges. The lifestyles of this energy animal might also advocate the superiority of a few aspect "wild" or hard to govern. Therefore, lions constitute hard-to-manage feelings like rage or terror.

As a spirit animal, the lion represents:

* Strength, aggressiveness, and strength

* The lion's spirit animal is regularly related to sentiments of aggression and rage which can be aimed each at you or at some other individual.

* Individual battle to govern those emotions

* Lion spirit animals provide you with a warning to a doubtlessly risky state of affairs or incident for your existence.

Peacock

The top of splendor is symbolized with the resource of the peacock. This stylish energy animal teaches self-love, dignity, and integrity similarly to the fee of face issues in lifestyles and the unknowable with self perception and courage. When the peacock enters your life with grace, you might be beginning a length of rebirth.

It's smooth to get over excited with the resource of the high satisfactory and run the hazard of going too a ways, as with something. Don't permit your self become haughty, useless, or unapproachable due to the fact the peacock totem encourages you to include self-love and self perception. The key's to keep a tremendous balance among arrogance and modesty.

Having a sturdy base allows for stability. Pay near hobby to the ft if you're studying the mysticism of the peacock. Our manual gadget and foundation are our feet. Peacocks have robust metatarsal spurs which might be sharp and famous as "kicking thorns." These are used by them to protect themselves from predators. They have sturdy legs, three powerful toes that face forward, and one sturdy toe that faces backward.

Rabbit

The implications of the rabbit spirit animal are extraordinarily nuanced. Due to the shy temperament of the rabbit, it's also related to fertility and creativity. In many cultures, the rabbit totem represents acceptable fortune and abundance. Thoughtful and imaginitive, folks that identify with the rabbit as their spirit animal may be fighting worry and dread.

Everyone has witnessed a rabbit prevent lifeless in its tracks earlier than bolting off on the identical time as a person passes thru. Rabbits are high-quality, tiny animals with few defenses. They are able to lighten up at the same time as consuming grass or dozing in their constant burrows notwithstanding treating everything as a functionality hazard. People who are rabbit strength animals may additionally moreover furthermore react timidly and fearfully in a same manner. They ought to experience uneasiness and be reticent in social settings. The rabbit totem encourages us to move beyond unfounded anxieties while however shielding ourselves.

Scorpion

Even even though we do now not usually experience like we've plenty strength or however recollect in ourselves, the scorpion represents the energy surely absolutely everyone own. It's essential for us to sometimes take a step into the darkish as a manner to become the human beings we want or want to be. When such takes vicinity, we turn to a friend like the Scorpion who can make stronger us at vital moments! Find out what the Scorpion manner symbolically and what feature it would serve in your existence.

The Scorpion normally stands for:

* Significant transformation

* Self-manipulate and tenacity

* Self enough

* Isolation and loneliness

* Aggression, repressed sentiments, or conduct

* The capacity to protect oneself from harm through undertaking combat, or to shield others through avoiding outdoor forces.

* High ranges of self guarantee

* Restraint and mastery

* Mental acuity, intelligence

* Achievement and force

Scorpion's symbolic importance may be each great and negative. Depending on the way you lease it. This animal teaches us to apprehend our inclinations, regulate them, and concurrently cause them to work for us in preference to in competition to us. We discover a way to discover our true self-identity, which has been stored hidden from ourselves for a totally prolonged duration, with the assist of the religious symbolism of the scorpion.

The first-class element of the Scorpion instructs us to analyze from errors, flip our weaknesses into strengths, and allow our ache to alternate ourselves into some detail better than we had been in advance than in preference to being scared of failing.

Sheep

The sheep spirit animal makes it possible as a manner to connect with your inherent innocence and sensitivity. When you stumble upon a sheep within the worldwide of spirit animals, whether or not in dreams or in the real international, it commonly stands for an innocent, childlike element of you. Spirit creatures that represent sheep can also constitute a propensity or need to in form in or study social norms.

The spirit animal of the sheep is cautiously associated with purity. This strength animal need to constitute a choice for brought natural, childlike elements in our lives. It may additionally evoke memories of instances or places even as we felt harmless, at the same time as lifestyles has elements of kindness, and it could encourage you to comprise greater of these traits into your current existence.

You may be experiencing feelings of vulnerability for your ordinary lifestyles whilst your spirit animal manifests as a sheep. The presence of the sheep indicates that you are feeling overwhelmed thru a sense of vulnerability and helplessness within the face of a tough scenario if the tone of the encounter is tinged with disappointment or terror, in particular if it takes location in a dream.

The presence of this strength animal moreover has a advantage in that it makes vulnerability more clearly defined. The presence of sheep might also suggest which you are connecting with a softer facet of your self, one this is open, willing, and available to experiencing in a kind, innocent way.

Squirrel

In the squirrel and its symbolism, there is lots more than meets the attention: As we move deeper and more deeply into its hidden meanings, we'd discover pride, playfulness, and expertise that could help us come to be greater modest in our non-public lives. The spirit of the squirrel demonstrates how real the adage "There is more to lifestyles than what we're able to see" is.

Significance of the squirrel

There isn't any unmarried description or angle for it, as there can be for maximum subjects. Typically, the squirrel stands for:

* Renew

* Flexibility

* Alter

* Spirit

* Jolliness

* Foresight

* Inventiveness

* Connection to the power of the floor and sky

* Appreciation

Squirrels are lovely animals with their very very own mythology and symbolism, just like many precise species. Even although, there may be one common issue among those shape of testimonies—the squirrel—that connects all of the worldwide locations. Because of its propensity to head back to the equal vicinity on the equal time every year only to discover that a few thing has changed, a few have dubbed it the "changer."

With the squirrel's soul inside us, we too may moreover look past our present constraints and get away from the monotonous forms of lifestyles. As we wake up and end up greater aware of our surroundings and ourselves, we study that the entirety is finally brighter and clearer to us.

Swan

If a swan crosses your route, she will help in guiding you inside the direction of more flexible techniques of thinking, respiration, and reacting to events. She needs you to recollect on your capability for foresight. Pay near attention on your woman intuition, intestine feelings, and premonitions. Keep your internal grace and splendor in mind. Let it come forth so that everyone can see it.

Giraffes

Giraffes aren't often notion of as spirit animals, but given their mild temperament and tall stature with long necks, they make a suitable spirit manual or strength animal. The giraffe can stand above special animals due to its prolonged neck. When it involves information our nature and the manner to interact with others, it has loads to inspire us. When it includes having empathy for others, giraffes haven't any problem the least bit, which inspires non-violence, real emotions, and properly-considered actions. The elements of tranquility, the heart, mindset-taking capabilities, or perhaps the growth of instinct are precious to the symbolism attached to this animal.

Although it could seem modest in the beginning, the giraffe is a sturdy spirit animal that would manual you for your route to identifying your entire capability. Continue studying to discover extra approximately the giraffe's which means and status as a spirit animal.

The giraffe is a creature wealthy in symbolism and which means that. Typically, it stands for:

* Softness and compassion

* Softness and compassion

* Elevation of the spirit

* Inner peace

* Inner peace

* The effect of or enchantment to exotism

* The effect of or choice to exotism

* Sincerity

* Awareness that grows progressively

* Harmony between sexual preference

* The capacity to stand out of the crowd

* You can advantage a deeper data of your very private individual traits or the styles in your life thru studying the most placing factors of the giraffe.

Your giraffe spirit animal has a superb effect on you; it calms you and evokes you to live in harmony with the area. It disturbing situations you to push tension and anxiety apart and technique existence with optimism. It suggests that you live calm. Before managing a disturbance, take some deep breaths. You will get away the typhoon along side your head held excessive as it will pass over you without touching you.

Your spirit animal is a giraffe, who teaches you the price of serenity and meditation. When giraffes are in corporations, check them. They are calm creatures. In some thing they do, they take their time. They continuously make slight bodily touch with exceptional giraffes.

You study from the giraffe that speaking does not require loud noises or complex shows. The giraffe's language isn't audible to human beings within the wild, except a toddler giraffe screams for assist, such even as it is in hazard of demise. Giraffes rent their postures to speak sooner or later of the day, and at night time they hum softly.

Wolf

In the sector of spirit animals, the wolf gives you a number of the maximum startling animal symbolism. The wolf's instinct, intelligence, need for independence, and facts of the value of interpersonal relationships are all delivered out thru its might. This animal may additionally moreover moreover represent a loss of agree with and a fear of being threatened. Pay heed to what your instinct is telling you whilst the wolf appears on your existence.

The wolf represents the following in the international of spirit animal

* Sharp mind and strong instinctual ties

* Hunger for freedom

* Display of powerful instincts

* Feeling worried, having little faith in unique humans or oneself

Positive connotations emphasize a sturdy bond together together with your instincts and intuition. On the down factor, the wolf may additionally need to face for a enjoy of hazard, a lack of self belief in someone, similarly to your private thoughts or deeds. This spirit animal moreover symbolizes keen intelligence in handling substantial problems.

Whale

The earth's dependable record keeper all through time is the whale. The whale is a totem that instructs you to take note of your internal voice, understand how your feelings have an effect in your each day life, and comply with your non-public convictions. When the whale enters your life, it can be time to take a better check in that you're, what alternatives and feelings led you proper right right here, and what you could do to put an prevent to the war and find peace. The whale is a photo of real reality for those who have it as their animal totem. They are nurturers and achievers who're conscious that life is extra complex than first appears.

The whale is regularly associated with creativity, internal reality, and emotion. These are some similarly interpretations of this totem:

* Holder of facts

* Physical and emotional healing

* Archivist of history

* Communication

* The charge of network and own family

* A renewal of emotion

* Calm energy

The story of Captain Ahab's pursuit of the large Sperm Whale called Moby Dick is the numerous most well-known cutting-edge-day money owed of the whale acting as a teacher. The artwork is permeated with superstition, an exploration of the huge mammal as a being of undetermined majesty, and the water as a automobile for transformation. Similar to how a person's inner fact, voice, and creativity can't be surely suppressed or tamed, the whale is a metaphor of that which cannot be with out issues vanquished.

Tiger

The tiger places a strong emphasis on unedited feelings and emotions within the realm of spirit animals. The tiger is a illustration of instinctual behavior, unpredictability, and self-self guarantee. This spirit animal can be a awesome in form for you in case you want to deal with life's conditions , trust your gut, and circulate fast whilst important.

Common tiger symbolism consists of:

* The tiger's symbolic which means facilities on courage, non-public electricity, and self-discipline.

* The shadow or aspect of yourself that you frequently try to conceal or reject.

* Anger or hostility directed at you or toward someone else;

*Unpredictability in existence, emotions, or existence;

The tiger has every fine and horrible connotations within the global of animal symbolism. Pay interest to the conduct this spirit animal reveals and the emotions you have got were given inside the course of it that allows you to well apprehend the message it has for you. It will lead you to a richer, extra embodied comprehension of this animal's significance on your existence.

Turtle

The turtle totem information encourages us to excursion our path in peace and to stay steadfast and at peace with it. Those who've the turtle as their totem or spirit animal can be advised to take a pause from their busy existence and are looking for round or inner themselves for extra grounded, extended-lasting answers. Turtles are slow moving on land but tremendously speedy and nimble in water. The turtle is a traditional illustration of the course to peace, whether or no longer or no longer it's far asking us to cultivate inner peace or a harmonious interplay with our environment.

The relationship of the turtle with the earth and earthly characteristics of staying power and stability distinguishes its symbolism:

* The Earth's and the arena's symbols

* The functionality to preserve calmness even inside the face of chaos and turbulence

* Pacing oneself and slowing down

* Persistence and resolution

* Emotional fortitude and comprehension

* Age-antique facts

The turtle is related to each the fluidity of feelings and the spirit of the water.

Panda

The panda is a sturdy spirit animal that evokes calm energy and tenacity. This animal photograph emphasizes the fee of having easy private obstacles that allows you to sense robust and anchored in existence underneath its cuddly and fluffy outdoor. If the panda is your spirit animal, you may have an emotional disposition and sense which you need big economic and physical consolation at the manner to experience snug to your existence. It will encourage humans who've it as their totem or energy animal to combine numerous components of their personalities right into a harmonious whole. This animal is symbolic of the functionality to find out a balanced and nurturing path thru lifestyles.

The panda is a representation of power and kindness. These are the general meanings related to this animal:

* Subtle power

* Peace

* Success and a satisfied thoughts-set on life

* Reference to Eastern wisdo

The symbolism of the panda also consists of personal and religious trends, which incorporates:

* Integration of polarized factors of your self, which consist of masculine and female energies

* Heart-focused strength and capability for nurturing

* The charge of feelings

* The capacity to set and acquire desires with staying power and calm solve

* The price of personal boundaries and private areas

Turkey

The spirit animal of the turkey is in element related to respecting the surroundings and the Earth. This totem animal, which stands for abundance, exhorts us to recognize all of our assets of sustenance, whether or not or not they will be intellectual, emotional, or spiritual.

The turkey serves as a mild reminder for us to establish non violent relationships with the land

and the environment and to view them because the cornerstones of our survival.

The Turkey totem can assist us discover the fullness of existence and learn how to be content cloth material with what we've got have been given in preference to obtaining more matters to make us glad.

The significance of the turkey is centered on our courting to the earth and the bounty it offers. Typically, it represents:

* Ampleness

* Relationship with Mother Earth and the land's spirit

* The Earth's blessings

* Reaping the rewards of your hard paintings and your efforts

* The fee of a community

* Generosity, cooperation

* Having plenty and being satisfied in lifestyles.

Panther

The spirit animal of the panther is powerful and shielding. The panther represents strength, courage, and heroism. You have a sturdy protector if the panther is your electricity animal. The panther represents motherhood, the general moon, and the may also of the night. This animal's totem pushes us to apprehend the strength lurking inside the shadows and to apprehend it in case you want to help us get over our worry of the darkish and the unknown.

What does the spirit animal panther suggest?

Common panther symbolism includes;

* Astral adventure

* Protection energy

* The woman image

* Rebirth and death

* Awareness of loss of existence

* Taking back your strength

* Knowledge of the darkish

* Aggression and electricity

Chapter 2: Spirit Animal, According To Your Zodiac Sign

There has long been a perception that every body born for the duration of a selected time period is associated with a specific animal. They have come to be called "spirit animals," and it's miles believed that they constitute your internal developments and man or woman. Astrologers have been able to confirm human beings's personalities thru zodiac signs and symptoms and signs whilst you do not forget that someone's spirit animal validates their human non secular electricity and desires. Below are t he spirit animals for every zodiac signal are indexed right here.

Aries

The hawk or falcon is your spirit animal. They are born leaders who're impulsive and continually willing to take the lead. Although they now and again display impulsivity, they constantly exude whole self perception. They also are very adaptive and passionate.

Taurus

The go through will resonate with Taureans. Bears represent energy and functionality, consequently Taureans are typically brave and robust those who can triumph over any venture with a decided mind. Because they experience relaxing of their familiar surroundings, they may become as gradual as a undergo.

Gemini

Although Geminis are taken into consideration to be very sociable, they will moreover be quiet and reserved at times. Therefore, they will have a character that fits a Black Panther. They are relatively domineering and fast on their feet. You're positive to offer them a 2nd take a look at all instances.

Cancer

Since Cancerians are meticulous and watchful, the Moose is a appropriate choice for his or her spirit animal. Whether they may be currently angry, disenchanted, or surely heat-hearted, you could in no manner tell what their mood can be like. These human beings are also quite sincere and normal.

Leo

In the exquisite possible manner, the Lion represents Leos. Leos experience taking middle degree and showcasing their talents to human beings spherical them so one can emerge as the alpha canine. Because in their beauty and self-assure, Leos are hard to overlook.

Virgo

Virgos are eager and extremely careful. As a give up end result, the Fox represents their individual because of their eager senses for movement and their intense caution. They are confident and composed, and that they've a totally first rate records of what they need and choice.

Libra

The Panda characterizes a Libran as lovely and lovable however with little hobby in extraordinary humans's activities. They experience engrossing themselves in their personal worlds. Additionally, Librans have a notable disposition and are a pride to be round.

Scorpio

The importance of this signal also can stem from the lethal Scorpio, however the snake is that this sign's soul animal. Despite being foxy, serene, and type, they will be as a substitute risky. If a person influences them in any way, they will not assume times in advance than harming them, however if they may be not afflicted, they will act gently.

Sagittarius

Red Pandas are the spirit animal of Sagittarians due to the truth they are wanderers with a carefree thoughts-set. They are absolutely consoling those who will in no way leave their loved one. They are type-hearted folks which are commonly inclined to help. They are capable of stay to tell the tale in tough and dangerous conditions way to their eager instincts.

Capricorn

Capricorns are analytical and sincerely clever human beings through nature. Like the Wolf, they cautiously don't forget all in their alternatives earlier than you decide, taking care to avoid making any errors. They have awesome judgment and might speedy defeat their adversaries.

Aquarius

Since it may be very hard to test what an Aquarius is thinking, they will be predisposed to have a very erratic thoughts-set. They are quite unbothered and unique of their life, similar to the Black Buck. They are able to with out trouble stay even within the most risky conditions thanks to this precise function.

Pisces

Pisceans are very giving and thoughtful of different people. Since they may be seen because of the reality the center of any company, just like the coronary coronary heart of the ocean, their man or woman is belief to hook up with fish. They are satisfied with their immediately circle of relatives and prefer sending brilliant power to others.

Frequently Asked Question

When people find out what a Spirit Animal is, all sorts of questions arise. They look for their Spirit Animal at that issue, which will increase extra questions. When they in the end get to meet their Spirit Animal, greater inquiries begin to float. Let's dive into the frequently asked question and their solutions.

What is My Spirit Animal?

I once skilled a tickling in my throat whilst appearing a shamanic spirit animal reading for only a new consumer. "Your throat chakra feels clogged and on fireside," I started out out speaking to her. You do not appear or sound ill. Frogs are all I can see round you. Oh, you are frightened of speakme inside the the front of corporations, and frogs have come to you as your spirit animal to assist. You want to now not be scared to sing your soul's melody, definitely as frogs aren't.

The horrific girl almost slid out of her chair, I expect. She became scheduled to supply a presentation at paintings the very subsequent day. Because she turn out to be imagined to cover for her unwell boss, she HAD to offer it. She emerge as hectic! She hadn't been getting any rest, and her throat end up beginning to damage. She had moreover observed severa Tree Frogs near her house.

The specificity of every Spirit Animal Reading varies. But in each Spirit Animal Reading, the right animal seems at the best time.

If a sitter's grandmother had a parakeet that she adored, the parakeet may appear in a mediumship reading as an evidential medium. Since the consumer modified into missing her grandmother, the parakeet appeared as a signal that grandma changed into safe and alongside side her preferred "Dexter" at the opportunity element.

All topics considered, it is vital for you to get to understand and growth a bond collectively collectively along with your Spirit Animal(s), as it is your spirit that need the help of the animal partners.

How Do I Discover My Spirit Animal

Finding your spirit animal is a breeze with the help of a spirit animal meditation.

If meditation isn't always your element, you can although ask your animal allies to expose your spirit animal to you through music, books, television, and syncronistic meetings with every human beings and animals. For instance, hedgehogs might be present anywhere. Then, as you revel in the pass-city bus, you notice a tattooed hedgehog! This is a non secular synchronicity. I Pray to the animal spirit publications to reveal themselves.

Discovering your spirit animal can push you to attempt new subjects. The following are some of the maximum common techniques to start:

* Look spherical you and inside the natural global. Pay hobby to how animals behave.

* Pay hobby whilst an animal makes an surprising appearance on your life or exhibits peculiar conduct; this can be a spirit animal looking for to get your interest.

* Be privy to repeated interactions with the animal, whether or not or now not they take

the animal's bodily or metaphorical form (as object or image)

* Examine one animal that stands out whilst you take a look at animal-associated books.

* Meditate on a specific animal you've got previously determined or with the general goal of discovering a spirit animal.

* Pay hobby to any animal-associated nightmares

Does Being in Nature Help Me Find My Spirit Animal?

Would or now not it's first-rate to encounter your spirit animal at the identical time as trekking up a mountain in Hawaii, at Machu Picchu, or within the Amazon Rainforest? Of direction! However, if you do now not plan on travelling to any a ways-flung places in advance than searching out your spirit animal, it or they may appear everywhere you're. My mentor as soon as advised me that she went on my first date with a person who labored as a trustee at an Eagle's Club. They headed to the membership to drink a few beer and dance, but it had already closed when they have been given there. Since he have turn out to be a member, he had the keys, so he opened the door so they might input. A huge Florida Black Snake grow to be wrapped across the door address when they grew to grow to be round to shut the door. Since Snake is considered one of her spirit animals and moreover a Native American and Chinese zodiac sign for Scorpio, She knew then and there that She have to marry him.

Conclusion, despite the fact that? Nature is you. So all you really need of the exceptional outdoor is to "move internal."

Is It Possible To Have Multiple Spirit Animals?

One of the maximum common inquiries regarding Spirit Animals is this one. The response is surely!

For the ones people who're touchy beings (specifically water signs Scorpio, Pisces, and

Cancer), our moods may additionally alternate considerably to the factor wherein we can also require the manual of a Lion nowadays however a Lamb the next day to tame the savage beast. All Bears proportion this trait, however extensively individuals who are extra touchy than the everyday Bear.

You will possibly have more than one Spirit Animal, as what you want for romance, help, consciousness, or healing at 20 may not be what you want for those things at 50. There are severa animal spirit courses for each season. Of route, I additionally frequently remark that I turned into aware of my spirit animal's affinity for bears even in advance than I determined out what a spirit animal have grow to be. The animal that looks most often once I'm harm or need assistance is the go through!

The amount of animals in a % or delight, or if numerous top notch animal spirit courses appear to you, may additionally additionally convey a sizable message or portent.

Will My Spirit Animal Stay With Me for existence?

A few do. Some people do not. The one element we're uncomfortable with is exchange, however the spirit global of animals isn't. When it's time for them to move away, consider your animal spirit courses to honestly will let you recognise. As smooth Spirit Animals enter your life that will help you, provide them gratitude and permit them to in.

Sometimes the operation of the Great Spirit is magic and thriller. But if we maintain our spirituality, the entirety always works out for the incredible.

What if I have become scared of my spirit animal or did not find it irresistible?

Never forget that Spirit Animals reply to our non-public spiritual calls for help. And our higher selves, our souls, constantly understand what we require for healing and re-balancing.

is acquainted with which animal may be an awesome high-quality friend. This sometimes consists of assembly our "Shadow Self" and searching into the gloom. It can be horrifying. Spirit, however, in no manner sends you a few element you cannot deal with or face.

Consider the case wherein your Spirit Animal manifests as a dolphin in a dream, at some stage in meditation, on tv, on social media, and so forth. That Dolphin, but, is unwell or hurt. From an emotional perspective, that can be sudden and adverse. But what if you hooked up a method that consumes you definitely? A dolphin that is unwell or hurt also can appear to you as a caution that YOU want to trade if you need to be healthy.

Remember the remaining time you felt unrestrained as you surfed through life? How lengthy has it been due to the fact you final laughed uncontrollably and played like a little one, just like a dolphin in genuine health? Now you see wherein that is going.

Consider a situation in which a female is a victim of an abusive marriage. Let's furthermore bear in mind that even as looking for your Spirit Animal, you run proper right right into a rabid gorilla. Can you discover the gender of the gorilla? If a lady, has Gorilla come to mention she will let you in being brave and sturdy sufficient to address the abuse, a few factor that involves for you? Has the male gorilla come to warn you that it's time to confront your worries, if he is?

You'll need to decide if the male or girl gorilla situation applies to you if you're in a equal-intercourse marriage.

How Can I Be Sure My Spirit Animal Is Real and Not Just a Fantasy of Mine?

You want to believe and be affected individual. Students often claim, "I completed the meditation, I desired for my Spirit Animal to appear in a dream, however nothing befell! Maybe there are not any animal spirit publications for me! There are infinite possibilities as to why the seeker's animal high-quality buddy or allies had been no longer there that day. Just unwind if this takes vicinity. The animal spirit realm loves you and needs the satisfactory for you; have faith in it. When human beings can also abandon you, your Spirit Animal will now not.

Why? Because in many strategies, your Spirit Animal is you.

Everybody is interconnected. Every one human beings is home to an elephant, bumblebee, and electric powered powered eel. When a koala endure passes away, a small a part of us passes away with it. Therefore, if a koala had been to appear as your spirit animal, it would definitely be a part of your self manifesting in the shape that your higher self is aware may be the most beneficial to you at that particular time. A nd feeling. You will "apprehend." Be careful no longer to mistake your Spirit Animal's visit as your creativeness and miss out on a effective contact with it.

What Does My Spirit Animal Want Me To Know?

Finally, Spirit Animals are welcoming to absolutely everyone. They are gift for certainly absolutely everyone. Additionally, they'll seem and talk with you in your "language." The animal spirit publications will technique you whether or not or no longer you communicate English, Spanish, or Swahili. Your spirit animal can be succesful to talk with you in a way that you can understand in case you talk super in massive phrases, avenue lingo, growing a music, softly, speedy, and so forth.

I met with a lady who modified into installing area a meeting for a friend who had these days misplaced her husband. I puzzled why she modified into surrounded through the colour purple. She claimed that the individual I have become imagined to observe for adores the shade pink, this is actually certainly certainly one of her preferred shades. She persevered with the resource of pronouncing that after she asked for a signal that she want to get in contact with me that morning, a Red Cardinal flew right away within the the front of her face! The animal spirit publications communicated with us in a language we have to each realize.

Why Did I See My Spirit Animal mendacity Dead?

You have a spirit animal named raccoon. One is lying vain at the facet of the road as you pressure with the beneficial useful resource of. You check approximately some specific lion being killed via poachers, and lions are your spirit animal. Your lovable Whale is floating within the deep ocean to your dream, lifeless.

Animals aren't fearful of exchange, as have become already stated. Typically, the presence of lifeless animals indicates approaching change.

Finding a deceased animal is scary sufficient, but while it's far your Spirit, Totem, or Power Animal, the intimacy of the scenario is hard to place into phrases. This animal, a thing of your soul's matrix, not possesses "lifestyles" in its earthly shape. How also can this be linked spiritually?

The first possibility is that your animal spirit guide felt the need to bypass on if your existence has these days expert a large transformation so as for a few different Spirit to artwork with the "new you." Please, but, do no longer panic. This does no longer endorse that your animal spirit guide gave up "himself." Your animal spirit animal had already made the selection to go away from this global, as a end result this indicates. Your animal spirit manual made the choice to move your direction subsequently in the course of its transition cycle as soon as that selection were made. This is a lovable instance of a trade message; your energy has changed, you have got were given superior for your development, and also you currently have evidence that you may go with assurance. If any other animal seems to you in the coming weeks or months, do now not be bowled over.

Another viable reason of why you'll likely find the mortal remnants of a Spirit, Totem, or Power Animal is if you're brushing off an essential truth this messenger has been looking to bring. This is a caution towards losing your self to irrational or unfavorable viewpoints that would essentially devour you.

Last but not least, this experience can be a sign of coming close to, dire risk. Whatever it is able to be—emotional, physical, or spiritual—hold your eyes peeled for the difference amongst fact and phantasm.

Chapter 3: How To Talk At The Facet Of Your Parent Spirit Animal

There are a few measures you could take in order to touch your animal even as you are in want of assistance from it.

First and primary, make sure you make an effort to unwind and middle yourself. This will permit you switch out to be more receptive to the messages which may be meant for you out of your kindred animal.

Once you have were given finished a state of serenity, you ought to motive to rid your mind of any thoughts and awareness to your breathing instead.

The subsequent step is to talk together along side your totem animal. You have the choice of doing this to your head or out loud.

Provide as masses detail as feasible at the trouble you are having and the purpose you're calling for help.

The subsequent step is to put together oneself to reap communications. These may additionally additionally come to you inside the shape of a idea, a picture, a sensation, or a few issue else else.

Pay interest to any signs or symbols which you be conscious round you for the motive that your animal accomplice may be in search of to talk with you via them.

Finally, make certain to thank your animal accomplice for all in their help and path.

How to determine what form of animal is your spirit manual

Your spirit animal may additionally inform others a top notch deal approximately who you are as a person and possibly offer clues about the spiritual route you have to absorb existence.

The first rate information is that there are a few specific techniques to decide out what sort of animal you have.

Consider which sorts of animals pique your hobby the most. This is one technique. Which of numerous animals do you pick out out out with the maximum? Which creatures, to your opinion, maximum as it want to be painting the essence of who you are?

Meditation and prayer are awesome techniques to hook up with the animal which you care for.

Turn your interest for your respiration whilst you close up up your eyes. It is crucial that you provide yourself permission to loosen up and easy your thoughts.

After you have were given performed a state of serenity, you have to supply attention to the question, "What type of animal am I?" Examine the concept that comes to your mind, whether or not or no longer or not it's a picture or a message. You can also locate it useful to consult a spirit manual or a better electricity for course in finding your animal totem.

Others genuinely located out a name to the cosmos, inquiring for route.

In order to discover their spirit guide, some humans may moreover even need to make a journey into the spiritual realm or speak with a shaman.

There isn't any one method this is excessive fine to carry you success in locating your animal. It is most important that you be willing to connect to some thing it is you're interested in.

The question now's, what shape of animal am I?

As became indicated earlier than, your guide animal is an animal that is symbolic of your non-public traits, inclusive of each your strengths and your flaws.

In addition to this, the animal in query is one with that you percentage a profound bond.

The preference of totem animal is likewise added about with the useful useful resource of one's cultural history. For instance, a studies that was executed in 2019 in Estonia concerning spirit animals indicated that the wolf turn out to be with the useful resource of a ways the maximum popular alternative (with 75 percent), followed with the aid of the usage of the undergo, the deer, the horse, and the eagle in that order correspondingly.

There are the ones humans who've usually had a strong connection to their animal companion. Others can be witnessing an animal that they've never even heard of, not to say visible.

It truly takes a couple of minutes of meditation on an character's favored animal for plenty souls to comprehend this.

We have compiled a listing of some of the most well-known spirit animals and the meanings related to them simply so the manner may be much less tough for you.

Bear is a spirit animal that represents staying strength, bravery, and strength.

The go through is considered to be a spirit animal as it embodies the qualities of strength, bravery, and perseverance.

If the bear is your kindred animal, it might be that you have a robust feel of self-strength of will and are a herbal leader.

You even have a excessive possibility of being exceptionally unbiased and having little staying strength for others who are not able to hold up with you.

Freedom, belief, and bravado encompass the Eagle as a spirit animal.

Many humans appearance to the eagle as a instance of bravery, independence, and vision.

If the eagle is the animal that you're feeling most related to, it is probably which you are an impartial man or woman who has a strong maintain close on who you're.

You also are possibly to private a extraordinary deal of bravery and a remarkable aim or direction in thoughts in your existence. After all, eagles are famend for having in particular sharp imaginative and prescient.

The spirit animal which means that of the butterfly is transition, trade, and new beginnings.

It isn't always unusual exercising to view the butterfly as a instance of metamorphosis, transition, and glowing starts.

If the butterfly is your spirit animal, it indicates that you are someone who is enormously flexible and who is constantly open to conducting new memories.

You're moreover possibly to have a first-rate sense of compassion and an intuitive capability, which goes hand in hand.

Independence, intuition, and self-self assurance are the guiding principles of the cat spirit animal.

People regularly look to the cat to represent their very very own revel in of autonomy, intuition, and self-warranty.

If the cat is your spirit animal, you are probably a robust self-reliant a person who is in track with their very very own innate statistics.

It's furthermore quite likely that you exude a robust experience of personal aptitude and feature a immoderate diploma of self-assurance.

The developments of gentleness, love, and innocence embodied thru the deer spirit animal

It is common for humans to appearance to the deer as a example of gentleness, kindness, and innocence.

If the deer is your spirit animal, you've got were given the capacity to be a person who is unflappable and type. You surely have a high opportunity of being really innocent and proudly owning a strong enjoy of personal integrity.

In a similar vein, the stylish deer is often regarded as a example of each thoughts and elegance.

In end, the deer is your spirit animal, which suggests that you have a sturdy connection to the herbal global.

The turtle is a spirit animal that represents knowledge, perseverance, and groundedness.

The turtle exemplifies the virtues of attention, persistence, and perseverance like few other animals.

It might be that you are a completely informed and affected individual character if the turtle is your spirit animal. This is due to the fact turtles are appeared to be mainly affected individual.

Additionally, it's miles feasible that you own a remarkable deal of persistence in addition to a exquisite lot of self-control. The vintage adage that "sluggish and normal wins the race" is some thing the turtle is well familiar with.

Keep going ahead, even though it is at a slow and constant price, simply because of the fact the turtle does, even in case you revel in like you're trapped in a rut. This is some element to preserve in thoughts if you experience like you're in a rut.

The tough employee and determined person of the Beaver as a totem animal

People often look to the beaver spirit animal as a example of tenacity and perseverance due to its artwork ethic.

Additionally, it's far connected to the standards of domestic, circle of relatives, and community.

The beaver spirit animal is referred to for its power, perseverance, and capacity to bear even in the face of adversity, making it one of the maximum powerful spirit animals. Beavers are considered with a view to adapt and thrive in lots of environments.

It is also viable that you are very adept at finding solutions to problems and that you have an entire lot of stamina.

The adaptability and tenacity of the possum as a spirit animal

The possum, every now and then known as the opossum, is an sudden desired in terms of spirit animals.

It is regularly used as a signal of model, it is linked to the reality that it is able to fake to be vain on the way to boom its opportunities of survival.

Additionally, the possum is well-known for its superb functionality to adjust to its environment. Possums are expert climbers and might regularly be decided suspended from the branches of trees in an inverted feature.

Because in their nocturnal lifestyle, possums are the maximum lively within the direction of the late hours of the night. In addition to being exquisite swimmers, they have got the ability to hold their breath for up to six mins at the identical time as submerged in water.

It is essential to bear in mind, much like the opossum spirit animal does, which you need to continuously be adaptable to wonderful activities and that there are instances while it is essential to behave as no matter the truth that you are lifeless so as to stay.

In addition to this, the possum spirit manual may additionally moreover moreover help you in gaining access to your very own middle of the night abilties and navigating hard seas.

Dolphin is a spirit animal recognized for its friendliness and sociable nature.

People that don't forget about the dolphin to be their spirit animal are normally concept of as outgoing, sociable, and enthusiastic those who are continuously up for a amazing time.

They are the supply of happiness and laughter everywhere they bypass, and they'll be often the life of the birthday party.

Additionally, dolphins have a popularity for being clever animals who are able to engage with each different and with human beings.

Those who've a dolphin as their spirit animal are normally professional at analyzing human beings and comprehending the feelings that they are experiencing.

They have an innate functionality to influence others, and that they almost usually have the capability to understand topics from severa views.

"Dolphin people" have a advantageous outlook on life, are empathetic inside the route of others, and are generally inclined to provide a assisting hand to parents which can be in need.

Fox spirit animal: one who's crafty and astute

Have you ever had the experience of feeling a deep connection with the foxy fox? If that is the case, then it is feasible that the fox is your spirit animal.

The fox has a reputation for being foxy and sly, and it's miles generally notion of as being a trickster because of its behavior.

In a extremely good wide kind of cultures, the fox is likewise appeared as a guide or a trainer, and it is believed that it can show parents which might be disoriented the manner to the direction that consequences in fulfillment.

People who bear in thoughts the fox to be their totem animal can also experience pressured to pursue modern endeavors, together with writing or acting, and can be inquisitive about delving deeper into their revolutionary selves.

The spirit animal of tranquility and spirituality is the praying mantis.

The praying mantis is frequently represented in famous way of existence as a serene and pious creature, one that has a reference to better powers.

It is said that they've the potential to educate us on the way to installation a connection with our greater superior selves and the way to maintain a wholesome equilibrium with the natural surroundings.

People who undergo in mind the praying mantis to be their spirit animal can also moreover need to sense forced to paintings in fields related to health or schooling. They also can have an interest in studying extra approximately meditation and other kinds of spirituality.

Spirit animal meanings of the polar endure embody tenacity, resilience, and remedy.

In many popular cultures, the polar undergo is visible as a signal of power, staying power, and tenacity. This idea is supported by means of way of the usage of the well-known way of lifestyles symbolism of the polar undergo.

Additionally, the polar undergo is seen as a defender of the helpless and a watchdog over the natural global in lots of cultures and beliefs.

People who take into account the polar go through to be their totem animal also can experience compelled to pursue employment inside the field of law enforcement or environmentalism. These humans may have an interest in sports sports that take area out of doors, such as trekking and tenting.

The lion as a spirit animal represents bravery and braveness.

Since ancient instances, the lion has come to symbolize majesty, power, and power because of its recognition because of the reality the undisputed "lord of the beasts."

The lion is a image of bravery and fortitude in masses of terrific cultures sooner or later of the location considering it's far believed to look at over the underworld.

People who receive as actual with the lion to be their spirit animal are probably to be interested in roles that require control or public provider, and they'll additionally have an hobby within the have a check of facts or mythology.

Spirit animal of the cheetah: swiftness and splendor

The cheetah is frequently used as a metaphor for swiftness, dexterity, and splendor.

It is thought that the cheetah is the first rate at hiding in simple sight, which has introduced approximately its association in severa societies with hunters and warriors.

People who keep in thoughts the cheetah to be their spirit animal can also sense pressured to pursue jobs in the appearing arts or athletics, and they will moreover have an interest

Spirit animal of the elephant embodies the developments of faithfulness, friendship, and thoughts.

The elephant is a spirit animal that is related with thoughts, intelligence, loyalty, and camaraderie. It is likewise associated with electricity.

If you turn out to be aware of as having an elephant as your spirit animal, it's far in all likelihood that you have a sturdy will and are inspired to obtain any endeavors you do.

You additionally may be an honest and dependable friend, in addition to having a excessive diploma of intelligence.

Elephants are recognized no longer first-rate for their intelligence but additionally for his or her large duration, which serves as a metaphor for enduring energy. People who recognize the elephant as their non secular animal normally have a robust feel of self-self assure and energy because of this association.

However, similarly to this, they will be capable of make clever use of their height and electricity, and they may be no longer afraid to shield others who're a good buy much less effective than themselves.

People which have this spirit animal usually have a number of compassion and cope with others, and that they placed the necessities of others beforehand in their very personal desires an entire lot of the time.

It's feasible that you may see matters that one-of-a-kind humans can't. In addition, elephants have a reputation for living very prolonged lives, making them an super example of the rate of enjoy and information.

The tiger as a spirit animal represents bravery and power.

It ought to come as no marvel that the tiger is taken into consideration to be one of the maximum well-known spirit animals.

The tiger is a powerful animal that personifies power, bravery, and unwavering treatment.

The tiger is your spirit animal, and as such, it has the capability to help you discover your internal fortitude and manual you via tough times.

When you're making a connection with your tiger spirit animal, you may discover that you experience an growth in yourself-guarantee and bravado.

A refreshed revel in of remedy and interest can come over you as well.

Your tiger spirit animal may additionally assist you discover the fortitude to confront tough situations head-on in case you discover yourself in a hard role.

This potential may be beneficial to you in lots of things of existence, on the aspect of your professional life, your personal relationships, or even the technique of self-development that you adopt.

There are high quality to be a few problems associated with the tiger. The tiger is every now and then concept of as a spirit animal that embodies unbridled rage and aggressive behavior.

If you word that you are performing in those strategies, it is vital to take a step again and take a look at in with the emotions which can be most deeply ingrained interior you.

Always preserve in thoughts that your tiger spirit animal is there to help and manual you; for this reason, positioned your religion to your intestine instincts and permit the tiger to expose you the way.

Wolf is a spirit animal that bestows sharp belief and comprehension.

Many cultures view the wolf as a signal of constancy to p.C. And own family further to open and sincere communication.

It is possibly that if the wolf is your spirit animal, you are a pretty dependable individual who places a immoderate significance on circle of relatives and pals.

It's additionally likely which you have sturdy verbal exchange competencies.

This enigmatic organisation animal is likewise a metaphor for one's innate skills of intuition and perception. If you've got were given a wolf as your spirit animal, it shows that you are very touchy for your surroundings and which you have an acute awareness and comprehension of the arena round you.

You have the capability to look topics that maximum humans do now not, and you commonly have a profound recognition of the area this is taking location around you.

You are enormously dedicated to the humans you care approximately and passionately protecting of them, but you furthermore may realise a way to have an splendid time and recognize life.

In a way quite just like that of the coyote, the wolf indicates that you are a powerful adversary, each in terms of your physical strength and your cerebral skills. This is some element that have to be taken into consideration.

In addition to this, you are self-assured and proficient, and you in no way fail to discover a way to any problem.

If a wolf is your spirit animal, it shows that you have a healthful dating with the untamed detail of who you're.

You do now not thoughts taking possibilities and placing your self in precarious situations. You are able to recommend for yourself and upward thrust up for the reasons which is probably vital to you.

You have tested which you are a survivor who is not fearful of troubles or checks. You never prevent going in advance and are generally looking for interesting new research.

The owl is a picture of an aged soul that is understanding past their years.

People whose spirit animal is the owl normally have a adulthood diploma that belies their age.

They are frequently people with "ancient souls" who've expert a brilliant deal in one or greater of their previous lives.

Rebirth is another concept that is connected to the owl spirit animal.

Due to the fact that owls are nocturnal animals, they'll additionally be interpreted to symbolize the shadowy a part of one's psyche.

If you discover that you are attracted to the owl as a spirit animal, it is probably time to face some of the fears and demons which you were heading off.

Alteration and new beginnings are also thoughts which is probably represented with the useful useful resource of the owl spirit animal.

If you have been feeling as like you're in a rut, the sighting of an owl can be a signal that it is time to make some adjustments to the manner you live your lifestyles.

Chapter 4: How To Discover Your Spirit Animals

The spiritual have an impact on of totem animals

To summarize, a spirit animal is any creature this is part of the animal international and that has been given non-public power with the useful resource of an man or woman. If you experience that the animal you have got were given selected possesses a positive trait, then that characteristic is possessed thru manner of the animal.

It is not unusual exercise to delegate non-public power through a totem animal. A totem animal is described as "an item (at the side of an animal or plant) functioning as a symbolic instance" of a positive characteristic, most customarily inside a selected prolonged own family.

A wild animal, however, is one that has "not been domesticated or tamed," steady with the definition of the term.

Spirit animals may additionally moreover show up themselves as any form of animal, and all of them supply with them a completely unique body of facts.

A incredible range of these creatures are related with a extra profound importance, supernatural talents, or a religious comprehension of a few type.

An embodied form of a religious manual is known as a spirit animal in first-class Indigenous spiritual practices. It is possible to make a connection with really one in every of your spiritual guides thru way of seeing them in the form of a acquainted animal. Our religious guides can also additionally moreover seem to us in a few component form that we're prepared to look them in.

You may additionally need to find out which you have a strong connection to a unmarried animal, or you will probable discover which you have a robust connection to severa exquisite individuals of the animal kingdom. Your animal manual(s) have a fantastic trait that has the functionality that will help you in navigating the disturbing conditions of life with a piece more ease, faith, and self-warranty.

Not exquisite which animal nice symbolizes you, or what it is trying to inform you approximately yourself through its representations? Here are a few net web sites that would assist you in locating out extra statistics.

Here are severa strategies that would assist you pick out your spirit animal:

1. Educate your self on the animal ties that run through your own family tree.

It is vital that the word "spirit animal" no longer be severed from its historic context because it has roots in the spirituality of Native American cultures. Because of the dearth of respect that many non-Indigenous human beings have for Indigenous way of life, many Indigenous human beings have asked that non-Indigenous human beings refrain from copying the traditional animal photographs decided on totem poles and pictographs.

Instead, devote a number of a while to studying the non secular importance that severa animals preserve inside the context of your very very own way of existence so that you may additionally moreover interact with the non secular importance of animals in a way this is genuine to you.

2. Pay interest to the dreams you have got been having.

Because our goals and our waking life are intricately intertwined, you want to make a be aware about any animals that seem in your dreams after which write them down the following morning. Is there a selected species of animal that appears more often than others?

three. Reflect on the techniques in that you had been associated with unique animals in the beyond.

Consider the animal that turned into your all-time desired at the same time as you were a infant, whether or no longer it have become a properly-loved doggy or a wild creature which you often encountered whilst you had been a great deal extra youthful.

four. Write for your journal approximately the creatures to which you have a strong connection.

Take a seat and exercise a bit meditation for five mins to calm your thoughts and make space for your intuition. Next, maintain in thoughts an animal that holds a totally critical vicinity on your coronary coronary heart. Ask yourself this query: If this animal have been my guardian, what existence instructions might probably it possibly be seeking to train me approximately my personal strength and inner energy? Taking a few minutes to jot all the way down to your mag approximately the reaction is usually recommended.

Carry out this interest a number of instances, using an assortment of severa animals for every generation. After some time has passed, you need to revisit your pocket e-book and decide which of the animals and the training it consists of most strongly reverberates with you.

5. Take a quiz.

If you have were given formerly finished things like analyzing animals, retaining a dream diary, thinking about on them, and dreaming approximately them, but you're however no longer tremendous which one exceptional resonates with you, finishing mbg's spirit animal quiz (underneath) can also additionally need to provide you with some smooth options.

After you have got were given identified your totem animal, you could then start to listen to it for guidance.

Animals often radiate a number of characteristics and skills that we may additionally domesticate and make extra use of in our very very own lives. If you're interested in a crow, for example, you could discover that channeling the continual hunter's power that it represents is beneficial to you.

Having a tangible depiction of your manual, collectively with a portrait, statue, or painting which you maintain expensive or adore, may be an effective method to supply to memory the tendencies of the animal that serves as your totem.

SUMMARY OF SPIRIT ANIMALS

Every time you're touched with the useful resource of your spirit animal, whether or now not it is thru direct interaction with it within the actual international, via viewing it in a photo, or thru taking note of a person else communicate approximately it, you've got the possibility to apply that experience as a reminder of the importance of the simplest-of-a-type traits it possesses.

A listing of common animals and the dispositions that outline them

The following is a quick rundown of the tendencies shared by using the usage of some normal animal courses:

Bear

The undergo possesses a sturdy emotional lifestyles and has a robust connection to nature and the first rate outside.

Butterfly

The butterfly is seen as a example of metamorphosis and development in a number of high-quality civilizations. It can outcomes modify to new situations and offers with them in a non violent and amassed way.

Cat

Frequently, the cat is a metaphor for inquisitiveness, freedom, and independence. Additionally, it has perfected the functionality to attend patiently.

Deer

The deer is a sensitive animal that possesses a immoderate degree of intuitive capability. It creates a balance among tenderness and splendor even as maintaining a level of self warranty and fulfillment.

Dove

The dove is a image of peace, benefits, and the begin of some difficulty new. It is an animal that has a effective outlook on life.

Dolphin

The dolphin is a picture of every merriment and enlightenment. It is a powerful device for every verbal exchange and unification.

Elephant

The elephant is an indication of intelligence, kindness, and the capability to apprehend religious principles.

Frog

It is often believed that the frog can also help in the recuperation of every bodily and highbrow wounds. This animal exemplifies the importance of regularly checking in with oneself and making peace with one's past a very good manner to be fully present in one's life.

Fox

It is said that the fox is the version for camouflage. It has perfected the art of separation and is able to increase in harmony with its surroundings.

Horse

The horse serves as a metaphor for one's motivation and fervor. It's pretty intention-oriented and effective on the equal time.

Hawk

The hawk is a metaphor for mind-set and the functionality to view a state of affairs from all angles. It is an animal that possesses a terrific deal of compassion and empathy.

Lion

The lion is a image of bravery and determination. It is a person who turned into born with a strong feeling of manage and authority.

Mouse

The mouse is a metaphor for the significance of paying near hobby to facts. It serves as a reminder to no longer gloss over the little info of life.

Owls have the precise capability to look subjects that awesome animals cannot. They understand the underlying significance of things and are capable of unearth existence's buried riches.

Peacock

The peacock is a photo of rebirth and rebirth via reinvention. It is aware that it is never too beyond due to choose out a one-of-a-kind method.

Turtle The turtle is a exceptionally religious animal that symbolizes the course inside the route of know-how, reality, knowledge, and quietness. The journey closer to those tendencies may be concept of as a journey within the course of knowledge.

Tiger

The tiger is a photo of intense and unfiltered sentiments and emotions. It has a strong intuitive capability and is quite real at following its intestine dispositions.

Wolf

The wolf is associated with statistics, primal urges, and unfettered independence. Primitive impulses take priority mainly special issues.

Chapter 5: What Are Spirit Guides?

The first-class way that I honestly have determined to answer the query of what spirit guides are is to factor out that Sprit—that strength that enfolds you, movements via you, guides and responds to you—is typically with you. There is in no way one 2nd in that you are separated from that Power. You are a part of it, and it's far an important a part of you. Even in the ones instances while you can enjoy truly by myself, you are in detail connected to Spirit.

The universe and all that is inner it is Spirit, which consist of you. You are a being of Spirit—a being of energy—and as such you are continuously associated with the whole lot else. This is a imperative guiding principle of shamanism that is now being examined via using technological knowledge.

Quantum technological knowledge proposes that the entirety is power; shamans say the whole lot is product of Spirit. There isn't any actual distinction between the requirements of

Spirit and strength, as explored with the aid of quantum technological knowledge. Their characteristics are a whole lot the same, if now not precisely so.

Except, possibly, for shamans, Spirit is alive.

What is Spirit?

Everyone has their private way of know-how Spirit. After many years of pursuing a method to that query, I truly have come to the notion that, for me, Spirit is "that this is more than I am." The mystery is the belief that a Power that encompasses all topics is also in element related to me, to you, to the whole thing. Although I do not have the phrases to offer an reason for how this is possible, I apprehend that it's far actual.

The belief which you are come to be impartial from Spirit is a delusion with a very short history, even in human phrases. The perception that you need to battle to find your way once more to Spirit—to be in reality really worth of such connection—is one of the key falsehoods of cultural socialization, and it has precipitated human beings a long time of suffering.

Through high-quality the past 2,000 to 2,500 years of the two hundred,000+ years of human lifestyles have humans divorced ourselves from an intimate dating with Spirit. As cultures have emerge as increasingly oriented to precise judgment and motive, the direct experience of nature, that is a vital conduit to Spirit, end up deprecated. The thriller of Spirit isn't always logical and prepared; it is intuitive and often chaotic. The language of Spirit isn't linear; it is symbolic and holographic.

It is also not actual which you need to have a specifically ordained middleman to talk with Spirit. You do no longer need a priest or a shaman to inform you what it needs you to concentrate. The shamanic journey, similarly to some of forms of meditation and prayer, can join you proper now with that Power. A maximum essential aspect in such communique is which you pay interest and apprehend the way to listen.

You are never on my own.

There is by no means one unmarried 2nd

whilst Spirit isn't with you.

Sit with that concept for a minute or . Let the feeling of the truth of it settle into your frame and bones.

Even on your darkest times, Spirit is typically present. How can it not be? You are part of it— immersed in it. That energy permeates your body and being all of the manner all the way all the way down to the cell diploma. You realize it, specially in instances of quiet solitude. Spirit is greater in detail linked to you than the air you breathe. In truth, in many cultures, Spirit and Air are the identical component. When you breathe in air, you breathe in Spirit. When you exhale, you breathe yourself into the vastness of everything this is.

Some people report this enjoy as despite the fact that someone is with them, frequently an entity of a few type. Depending on their way of existence or revel in, they will revel in as even though they're being visited by an angel, a spirit, or a departed cherished one. Some additionally document a sensation of peace or "oneness." All of those descriptions are valid because of the fact there may be no manageable label for such reviews. They are basically transcendent. It is in these moments while reference to Spirit could be very sturdy.

To enjoy this is truly pretty smooth. The project is to preserve directly to the feeling, to the expertise of the fact of it in everyday life. That is why a consistent exercising is needed a good way to make that connection and discover ways to weave Spirit into all the arenas of your existence. A effective way to do that is to objectify the feeling, to make it actual.

In shamanic circles, that is carried out through cultivating a courting with spirit publications, such as animal courses. As I get to realise Wolf, and he gets to understand me, a kinship is stable through the years. Through that relationship, I get to apprehend extra about how Spirit works and the way it interacts with me at once on a second with the aid of 2d basis.

In journeys, publications come to you to hold messages from Spirit, regularly in response to a question you have got got were given or an hassle about that you would like a few clarity. Most commonly, the verbal exchange isn't in phrases, even though it might be. However, even in case you bought terms, recognize that the phrases themselves aren't the whole thing of the message.

Words and language are very confined of their capacity to keep facts. Symbols are a long way extra green. That is why the solution or reaction of Spirit in your cause for journeying may additionally unfold as a scene or movement. And, as most journeyers recognize, the courses do now not certainly "talk" to them. Most of the time, the communique is greater like telepathy. You genuinely apprehend what the guide is asking to talk.

Conversation with Spirit is facts-wealthy. It isn't always frequently in phrases, virtually. If what Spirit had to inform you was transmitted linearly, as in phrases, it might take a completely long time to get the message. That is an important purpose that most messages from Spirit are inside the shape of symbols.

Even the guide who brings the message is a critical a part of it, as nicely. That Wolf includes the message in place of Serpent is sizeable. So, it is crucial to have a study the ones publications—their conduct, traits, the entirety you may—because of the reality they're key additives of the message, too.

As with dream interpretation, symbols offer many unique layers of that means, and expertise them can take some time. It is like walking with oracles—Tarot, I Ching, Runes, and masses of others. Any card in the Tarot deck, for instance, is full of because of this in itself, given all the type of its included symbols.

However, context is likewise crucial. Where it falls inside the unfold is essential to statistics how the cardboard, with all of its symbolic language, is related to the query or issue available. Even with a one or card draw, the because of this of the card is muted without the context of the cause for the drawing and the relationships a number of the playing cards drawn.

The wealthy language of the image, in addition to its context, are both crucial keys to interpreting the message. So it is with strolling with adventure courses. Yet, the shamanic way of strolling with animals and wonderful beings as courses is even more complex due to the fact those messengers are alive.

Spirit is holographic, and messages from Spirit reflect that holographic complexity. It is said that "a image is well worth a thousand terms." How a bargain more so a living photo than a image!

Notice that the ones publications are not similar to dream symbols as maximum humans have come to take into account them. There isn't any one-to-one relationship of a guide to a particular that means. There is a ebook called 10,000 Dreams Interpreted, written in 1931 through Gustavus Hindman Miller and up to date in 2012, which is essentially a dictionary of dream symbols and their meanings. This and similar books can be useful resources, despite the fact that they will be pleasant not considered definitive.

Other books that provide beneficial insights into animal traits embody:

Animal Speak, by means of Ted Andrews

Animal Wise, moreover through Ted Andrews (paperback most effective)

Animal Spirit Guides, by means of the usage of Steven Farmer, Ph.D.

While there are numerous specific such property to be had, those are the 3 that I preserve to rely upon. The key motive is they do now not inform the reader what every animal way, however interest rather on its tendencies. Within the animal's trends lie clues to the purpose that unique being carries the message.

How is Wolf different from Serpent, or Falcon, or Oak?

The great manner to technique the ones descriptions is to take a look at thru them and allow your body recommend what's applicable to the message for you at the time and for the problem. Much of the outline also can have little to do together along with your modern-day situation or query. Pay attention via and large to what catches your popularity, and wherein you experience that a phrase, word, or observation is in particular relevant.

Remember, this is a verbal exchange from Spirit for you, now. Sparrow for you on this trouble can be very certainly one of a kind from Sparrow on every other issue in a selected time. And what others say approximately it's miles for them, not for you, until their statement feels in alignment with the purpose of your hassle and the message.

We will delve extra deeply into the challenge of know-how adventure guides all through this e-book. For now, it's miles sufficient to understand that connecting and operating with courses—animals and others—are crucial methods that you could communicate without delay with Spirit, with that inner understanding this is your birthright.

Are These Guides Real?

Shamans, who are very practical if quite mystical, can also say so. To them, there may be little difference some of the purposeful components of ordinary fact and the efficacy of non-normal fact. In fact, the two are very complementary, and it could be that they can't be separated. Our "actual" international is in element interrelated to the possibility.

Make no mistake about this. The Spirit World is as real as the one you live in each day, and the denizens of that worldwide are, too. If you do now not apprehend this, or forget about approximately it, then you will discover your journey enjoy an increasing number of tough. It is as despite the fact that you welcome a stranger onto your land or into your own home. If he behaves disrespectfully or takes your hospitality without any consideration, you may probable now not be so welcoming in the future.

This has came about to pretty a range of expert journeyers. They will be inclined to note at the equal time as their journey experience "dries up," or their guides start now not to expose up for them. Now, this isn't always the most effective reason for such activities, but it is a very real opportunity.

When you meet a manual, you constantly want to be respectful. In my experience, few if any publications need to be worshiped or positioned on a pedestal. In truth, you'll probable question whether or now not this shape of being is a guide for you in any respect. Remember, now not all the denizens of the Spirit World are there for you. They have their personal lives, their very personal volition, and may not have some issue to do at the facet of your adventure revel in.

Notice, too, that animal guides and messengers are referred to as with the aid in their very very own spirit name: Wolf, instead of a Wolf or the Wolf. This is because of the fact the being turning into a member of you is the spirit of the animal, the living archetype. So, as you figure collectively together with your animal courses, teachers, and messengers, recognize that each one of the beings they constitute moreover be part of you.

While animal and one of a type courses are messengers and teachers, they not often keep themselves as advanced to human beings, if ever. Now, they'll tease you or poke a laugh at yourself-significance, but it'll no longer be as an expression of "I am higher than you." It is probably to educate you some thing about your self which you need to take care of.

So, are adventure courses and instructors actual? I advise that you permit for the opportunity that they're, and via your personal journey enjoy, decide for your self. Even so, it makes plenty of sense to be respectful.

Why "Animal" Guides?

For tens of lots of years, humans and animals had been together as every enemies and buddies. If for no person-of-a-type purpose, it grow to be not that prolonged in the past in archeological time that people have been an critical part of the food chain: we ate them, and that they ate us. So, it makes first-rate feel that our near physical relationships may be mirrored thru our near religious relationships.

Humans started out to domesticate animals in the Mesolithic length (20,000 to 9,500 BCE). However, signs are that puppies have been the primary to work cooperatively with people almost 33,000 years in the beyond. Still, the most lively attempts to cultivate goats, sheep, farm animals, and unique farm and art work animals befell starting round nine,000 BCE.

Domestication takes many generations to carry out, as it takes place at the genetic diploma through selective breeding. So, human relationships with animals involves genetic exchange in every human and animal species. In a feel, we have evolved together over hundreds of years.

And but, it seems the connection can also run even greater deeply.

Several years ago, a family of opossums took up residence in our application room, this is spoil unfastened our house. I positioned them by using accident, hiding inside the lower back of the washing tool. It became very cold, so it seemed appropriate to let them stay. Within some days, they moved on.

We have an outdoor cat, who without a doubt refused (on the time) to return again internal, as she did now not similar to the trendy indoor cat. Of necessity, then, we fed her outdoor. Of path, that added other critters, which includes raccoons, to the family. I started out to place the cat's meals up on a small, 0.33 shelf of the baker's rack that we used for gardening equipment. The outdoor cat have to eat on the bottom shelf, then I might circulate the bowl as an awful lot as the higher shelf.

One night, I heard some of noise outdoor. When I went to investigate, I noticed a young opossum, probable one of the ones that sheltered in short in our software program program room, consuming from the cat meals bowl. It hissed at me and scurried away, climbed head-first down the leg of the baker's rack, and disappeared. I then moved the bowl to the pinnacle shelf, which come to be very narrow, really. I determined that the opossum probably could not achieve it, and I became in element accurate.

The next midnight, I heard scuffling noises out of doors over again. This time, the opossum changed into at the 0.33 shelf, apparently in search of to discern out what to do. It hissed at me again, and backed to the far end of the shelf, but did not run away. On impulse, I placed a few bits of cat food at the shelf and stepped back.

After some time, to my pleasure, the opossum crept beforehand and ate a number of the meals, after which withdrew. I modified the meals, and it got here ahead again to devour. We did this for some time until it both got spooked or whole and scurried head-first down the baker's rack leg and once more disappeared into the darkness.

This went on every night time for some time. Eventually, she might permit me stay close by at the same time as she feasted on the cat meals. She can also need to although now and again hiss and display me her lengthy, curved, and really volatile teeth. Yet, she in no manner bit at me.

During the kind of visits, I started out to wonder about the connection that we regarded to be growing. The call Guinevere got here to me one night time time, and I discovered out that I had no concept of the opossum's gender, even though it had constantly felt woman. So, Guinevere it was!

Then one night, she permit me contact her. I had in no way felt opossum fur. It is as stiff as a boar's hair brush, lengthy, and unruly. I brushed her once more lightly with my fingers, know-how instinctively that her head and tail have been very heaps off limits. I petted her for handiest a short on the equal time as, feeling very honored, and not seeking to push too a long way beyond that intimate boundary.

While I knew that I changed into growing a shape of special bond with this feral creature, I had no concept how she might also view her relationship to me. That is, until our ultimate stumble upon.

My family and I once more domestic from shopping one afternoon, numerous months later. I had now not visible Guinevere for pretty a while and had come to be involved as to her properly-being.

As I closed the car door, I observed her drawing close to me from the carport. I knew some component was wrong. Not nice become she out at some diploma inside the afternoon, which in no way came about because it is fairly unusual for nocturnal beings to be out inside the town daylight, she changed into scooting along on her right side.

It came about to me that she might have been hit with the useful resource of a vehicle, or attacked via one of the puppies inside the community, but I had no idea. Yet, she had simply been injured considerably. She stopped severa feet away, lying on her thing, and we looked at every wonderful for numerous mins.

I did now not realize what to do. Should I try to take her to a veterinarian, and what have to seem then? The final results of calling animal control seemed no higher. I changed into ill-ready to nurse a wounded opossum. After a minute or so, in spite of the truth that, she grew to become and scooted into the out of doors, into the comb, after which she have become lengthy beyond.

I am glad that she came to go to me in her final hours, that she had moreover bonded with me over the diverse weeks that we have been together. She came to say, "Goodbye."

It appears to me that, if an city dweller, inclusive of I, can shape a nice courting with a wild opossum, the connection that we've got got with animals runs very deep, certainly. She modified into honestly not domesticated, nor modified into she tame. Still, the relationship in our biologies held the easy capability for a meaningful connection.

Certainly, people shape relationships with the Stone and Crystal People, the Plant People, the severa elements, and other beings. I frequently journey to go to the Thunder Beings once I are searching for insights into the weather. All of these are perfectly legitimate! It isn't my motive to denigrate any of them. And however, I do believe that our shared flesh-and-blood biology and genetic evolution form a herbal matrix thru which we shape a completely specific archetypal bond with animals.

ANIMAL GUIDES

It is very tempting and natural for humans to categorize and pigeonhole pretty much the whole thing. Doing so is a key manner that you make experience of your revel in and your global. However, strolling with spirit publications and instructors defies this manner of organizing the area of non-everyday truth.

In the adventure experience, as an instance, a particular being not frequently "approach" the same aspect for particular humans or in outstanding contexts. We found within the very last chapter that Skunk may also supply a specific message or belief to you in a single example and a very particular one in some different. Yet, most customarily, Skunk has some component to do with placing or retaining barriers.

This financial disaster proposes a based manner to artwork with animal courses by searching now not at the animals themselves, however to how they could relate to you—or how you may relate to each different. Each of those perspectives consequences in a form of shamanic adventure revel in, as well as strategies that you can integrate them into ordinary life.

Journey Guides and Allies

These remarkable, smart animals are the guides of shamanic touring. When you adventure into the Spirit World, they may commonly accompany you, display you spherical, defend you, and offer solutions for your questions—or come up with a route on your journey.

There is a completely realistic element to going for walks with Journey Guides. In the beginning of your adventure, whilst your guide appears, tell it as really as you can your reason for the adventure. Once your guide knows, turn the adventure over for your manual to influence the manner. Your feature then becomes that of an active witness and player, instead of the writer or director of the revel in. In that manner, the Journey Guide let you depart in the back of the machinations and expectations of your analytical mind and circulate into the magical and stimulated journey into Spirit.

You will probable come upon literally dozens of animals in shamanic journeys. Often, those animals type themselves out in line with forms of enjoy, know-how, and recovery favored. Not they all might be critical for you longterm.

Although you will growth a courting with a few key Journey Guides in time, you can find that positive ones of them seem to facilitate unique types of journeys. Some will appear no longer often, or possibly most effective as quickly as, in keeping with your want at the time.

Remember that the beings that you meet can be animals, plants, stones, humans, legendary creatures, and greater. Avoid restricting your self to any preconceived belief of what they is probably for you.

A really particular manner to keep in mind locating publications is the identical way which you discover friends and assemble relationships with them through the years. This is especially true in on foot with Journey Guides and Allies

When you go to a party in which you do now not realize many humans, for instance, you would probably search around and get an effect of the kind of people present. You might be inquisitive about a number of them, at the same time as others you may not. You might discover someone which you would love to technique for a communique, whilst others won't seem interesting.

In the course of the nighttime, you possibly should have had a number of conversations with some of humans. You should probably experience a connection with a number of them. It is probably that the ones becomes pals. And in time, some of those pals may additionally come to be precise buddies. Perhaps one or of these "right buddies" will become "notable pals." In our analogy, the ones might be what you may communicate over with as spirit courses.

Developing relationships with Journey Guides can be very much like that, with the exception that, for hundreds, there is a kind of initial "spark" upon meeting. When the guide appears, you may get the experience that there's a few element unique or fascinating approximately it, as one of a kind from the others. These encounters may be very compelling and well worth revisiting over the years.

For example, Wolf has prolonged been a principal guide for my trips, genuinely due to the truth the very starting of my exercise. He confirmed up right away, and began to teach me in touring. In the early days, he may additionally need to show up with a harness like that associated with seeing-eye puppies. He ought to no longer lead me everywhere until I took hold of the manage.

I located this pretty disturbing and frustrating, and it went on for a long time. Eventually, in a unmarried journey, he have become all at once off the path that we had been following and quite virtually dragged me up the steep slope of a hill. At its summit, I need to see the maximum wonderful vista! I even have end up enthralled nicely beyond description.

When I appeared down, Wolf modified into gazing regularly into my eyes. The harness turned into prolonged past. Then, I determined out that the harness indicated that he modified into critical me "in which I couldn't see." And that became authentic. In the early days, I changed into pretty slender-minded, analytical, and literal. It may additionally have been very tough for Wolf to have led me everywhere that I would possibly no longer agree to move—that I did no longer accept as true with changed into feasible or real.

This statistics become not a few thing that I would possibly have without problem not unusual had Wolf surely informed me so. It become a few element that I had to find out for myself thru direct experience. When this form of detail takes place for you, you may recognize beyond doubt that the shamanic journey exercise is as real as any education you've got got ever had.

This is how Journey Guides frequently paintings.

Guardians

You will possibly stumble upon Journey Guides who characteristic as Guardians for you on a number of your travels. Most often, you may apprehend them with the useful resource of manner of ways they experience to you: protecting and nurturing.

Some journeys include visiting locations in that you might mainly be afraid or at least anxious. Shadow Journeys, for example, lead you to deliberate encounters with beings that have a tendency to inspire tension or perhaps worry. Guardian allies make extraordinary additions on your travelling business agency.

However, their presence does not suggest that there may be danger nearby. In more than a decade of touring and training the exercise, I in reality have in no way encountered a being that I could remember of any real risk to me or my well-being, or that of my college students. We will visit this within the speak of Shadow Animals rapidly.

Guardians are commonly genuinely that. They reduce your anxiety degree with the aid of using way of their very presence. You experience more stable because of the truth they're with you, as a younger one may also on the identical time as travelling with a discern or depended on person. Traveling on my own into new or wonderful territories may be worrisome. It is good to have a strong and potentially fierce accomplice.

These allies seem in an entire lot of office work. Eagle flying overhead can also feature a lookout, as an example, whilst Panther walks ahead or beside you on alert. One journeyer is frequently followed thru a huge Tree, as it solidly protects his lower lower returned!

Some traditions advocate that one ought to normally have a Guardian even as visiting inside the Middle World. According to this manner of questioning, there are numerous sorts of spirit beings that one should encounter on the ones journeys, now not all of which are first-class. My wellknown method to the workout is much less fear-primarily based absolutely.

Though I do apprehend that there are darkish energies to cope with within the ones journeys, as with a few kinds of spirit paintings in normal reality, I even have trouble with the notion of evil entities or what are referred to as demonic forces. Such beings that I encounter appear to me as wounded and in need of restoration as a substitute.

Nonetheless, I constantly sense extra safe and confident in dark locations with Panther at my side!

Like different journey courses, Guardians have a propensity to trade, regardless of the fact that a few relationships are longer lasting than others. Falcon, whom I speak with as my Totem, also serves as a mum or dad as he circles above. And frankly, his appearance in normal life usually brings a experience of both wonder and peace.

Teachers

You will genuinely encounter one or extra beings who serve as Teachers, who greater immediately provide knowledge or insights. While the speak of the excessive content fabric cloth rate of symbols stays actual, it is sometimes useful to have a communique with an first-rate buddy who clearly solutions your questions.

Journeyers often discover that the ones Teachers appear in a given region, in preference to being a touring accomplice. For instance, one individual located that his coaching nice friend, an elder Native American, generally seems while he is sitting on a fallen tree in his Lower World journey center. Another located that her Teacher, who she calls Shaman Woman, lives in a hard-hewn hut interior a remarkable wooded area.

As a massive generalization, you'll in all likelihood go to in which the Teacher is, in region of the Teacher coming to you. You may additionally furthermore discover, as many do, that those allies are usually extra Human beings than Animal beings.

Teachers have their very own characteristics and types of education, simply as instructors do in ordinary fact. They can be stern, or appear impatient, or they'll be deeply loving and simply accepting. In each case, they're exactly who they need to be for you.

Of direction, the individual of their appearance and your interactions and dating with Teachers show you a brilliant deal about your man or woman. Who and what they may be and the manner they behave are properly actually really worth attending to as vital factors of their lesson, as well. Remember, no longer something of non-normal fact and the Spirit World is simple and linear. Everything is holographic and statistics-wealthy.

There also are many commonalities in encounters with Teacher allies. For example, shamanic education is most often done through guiding the scholar to recognizing that she or he already is aware of the solution to many questions. "You already recognize..." is a phrase that journeyers pay attention quite regularly.

Relationships Rather Than Roles

These are a few key allies that you could maximum in all likelihood come across in your trips. Remember that those are lessons of relationships, now not assignments of any precise animal to a given position. Any being may additionally interact with you in any of these or specific relationships, and who they'll be to you method little or no longer something if accomplished to others.

If you are a healer, you can probable find that one or extra publications will paintings with you in ordinary fact as Healing allies. You can choose out such allies in journeys and get in touch with on them to be with you as you allow Spirit to go together with the go together with the flow through you to the healing of your clients.

And those allies aren't usually constrained to the Spirit World. If you're a trainer in regular life, for instance, you may discover that a Teacher every now and then speaks via you. You may additionally have already got had the enjoy of expressing some element particularly insightful to your students. But at the same time as asked to copy your self, you can now not be able to go through in mind what you said surely seconds earlier than. In these instances, your Teacher joined within the discussion!

Finally, simply as your journey is probably distinct from unique human beings's journeys, your relationships to the beings and allies which you meet can be specific to you. As you still explore your relationships with the beings working with you in the ones roles, bear in mind that what all people else says about them are actually their very personal critiques. They can be exceptional insights, but they will be only beginning factors or signposts on your private records.

Totem Animals and Spirit Names

Most regularly, while people say that they need to recognize what their "energy animal" is, they are expressing a desire to have a unique relationship with an animal being that may be known as a Totem. In order to apprehend this form of dating, it is beneficial to do not forget that you are basically strength.

Consider that, as an strength being, you have a remarkable vibration, like a tone. Your power frame sings, in a manner, and that vibration falls inner a specific spectrum that may be identified as human.

Now, indoors that massive spectrum of humanness, there are versions, of path, and a number of the tones harmonize with every one of a kind at the equal time as others do not. You normally commonly generally tend to get at the side of a few people and no longer with others. This concept is in our language: "He absolutely doesn't resonate with me," and "I get a peculiar 'vibe' from her."

Some humans appear so comparable that they'll appear to others to be related, even though they may be not. People may additionally constantly be compelled for someone else. Also, you have probable met a couple of person whom you may call with the useful aid of the wrong name, due to the fact the call they let you know seems in some way now not to "in shape" them, at least now not on your view.

In all of those instances, what is going on is that your energy frame is reacting to the vibration of their electricity frame. Of path, this takes area outside of your conscious reputation. Nonetheless, the effect is plain.

Other beings vibrate as well, of course, despite the fact that animals, plants, stones, and others can be said to accomplish that at a selected frequency than humans. In this view, the animal spectrum is as an alternative in the direction of human than is that of flowers and stones. This is probably every other motive that human beings have a propensity to narrate to animal courses extra than others.

(That being said, you in all likelihood understand people who do relate to Plant People or Stone People greater effortlessly than animals or human beings. There is a extraordinary range in all of this!)

And, as there may be model inside the spectrum among humans, there's version within the animal spectrum, as well. Skunk, Wolf, Eagle, Dolphin, Spider are all very particular, no longer only bodily, however moreover in how their vibrations revel in and within the way you harmonize with them.

That is the key to knowledge relationships with Totem Animals.

I realize, after a few years of exploring this question, that I am a member of the Bird Clan. For me, this is easy. My Totem is Falcon, and I are looking for advice from this as my spirit call. I actually have an extended and tremendous story about how this dating came to be that might take thousands of this chapter to tell.

So, from this power/physics mindset, the vibration of my strength frame falls close to the spectrum of Birds, and maximum mainly within the path of the predatory raptor. Falcon is a most satisfactory-tuned illustration of that precise vibration, even though Hawk is likewise very close to. (In fact, human beings every so often speak with me as Hawk or experience me as Hawk in journeys and dreams.)

I actually have pals and fellow journeyers whose spirit Totems are Oak, Amethyst, or even Carrot. These energies fit their personalities well and, more importantly, experience right.

You, too, have a special vibration, of course. You, too, have a Totem this is maximum likely an animal for motives we've got got and will hold to discover.

Relationships with Totem Animals have a tendency to be longterm, genuinely for years. However, they're capable of exchange, mainly as you convert every in age or through enjoy. If your vibration adjustments enough, you might not have a vibrational harmonic with a specific being.

For instance, in a few cultures, the name given to children is a mirrored picture in their Totem at delivery, instead of being assigned to them as a manner of tracing their lineage. Then, as they become older and mature, their call in the tribe can also change. Names may additionally moreover change because of the fact the cease quit end result of a primary lifestyles occasion: a existence-changing trauma, massive non secular evolutionary leaps, or as an honor for a valorous act.

Our EuroAmerican lifestyle is primarily based on a splendid and extra ordinary naming scheme, of course, but that is associated with tracking circle of relatives traces for categorization functions for the maximum detail. Still, a person's common name expresses some of their important vibration.

Some humans that I recognize have located new names as a way of fostering change in themselves, and this is flawlessly legitimate. A pal, River, did if you want to deliver a extra flowing and effective electricity to her existence, and it does suit her nicely! Every time that call is spoken, it reminds her of who she desires to be (or genuinely is), and having that tone related to her does exchange the vibration of who she is within the international.

Another buddy changed his name legally to erase his connection to his beyond and to set a brand new tone for his future. It did so in a effective and sudden manner. The new call come to be a clean tonal expression of his nature, and it became even greater so.

Your call is a sturdy expression of who you're within the ordinary worldwide. Your spirit name is the same in the spirit worldwide, as nicely. Your internal understanding of that energy is maximum in all likelihood why you is probably very interested in information what your Totem is.

It is also why Totems can be hard to become aware about. Most human beings find out that they've a sturdy attachment to a selected animal or notable being, and that they do now not need to find out that it's far particular than they preference or anticipate! That attachment can make the hunt very tough.

Let me positioned a number of that trouble to rest. The truth that you could have a strong feeling or affinity for a selected animal is an expression of your connection to it, and this is crucial. Whether or no longer that being is "your Totem," it is a large manual for you, at the least.

Chapter Four will endorse a particular adventure that will help you grow to be aware of your Totem. Know earlier, despite the fact that, that this form of adventure is a quest and not continually a revelation. It is also an odyssey a good way to engage every of your worlds: spirit and ordinary realities.

Finally, despite the fact that the connection with a Totem animal is longterm, it's going to likely exchange as a part of your personal evolution. Often that change can also appear tough, as it would on the same time as a pleasant friend actions away. When the ones transitions appear, it's also the Totem that permits the method. And you may discover that the Totem Animal stays somewhere nearby.

After all, you still have harmonic vibrations.

Messengers

As the impact and messages of Spirit aren't limited to the Spirit World, neither are animal guides. Messengers supply us inspirations and guidance from Spirit to which we want to pay hobby in our modern situation. We come upon those Messengers each in the non-normal international of the shamanic adventure AND in normal lifestyles.

Many humans have had this kind of revel in. However, if they do not recognise the importance of such encounters, they'll without troubles regard them as old style, despite the fact that possibly interesting, coincidences.

When you're visited in a weird manner via an animal, insect, bird, or one in all a kind creature all through the day, pay hobby. Remember that Spirit is constantly speaking with you, and it could be that the animal is a Messenger for you. When it captures your hobby for any reason, ask your self—and it—what its message is probably for you at that factor and in that vicinity.

The meanings of messages brought with the aid of way of these allies may be understood in exactly the same manner as with journeys. Consider the animal itself, the context of the stumble upon, and what it's miles doing as clues to the symbolic that means.

What sort of animal is it? What is it doing, precisely: gambling, strolling, chattering? Is it by myself or with others? What does your intuition assist you to know; what's your guess about what the Messenger is trying to speak?

For instance, one afternoon I located myself developing irritated as I tried to accomplish a few art work obligations. Nothing regarded to be getting finished. I stored getting interrupted and having to begin some tedious, linear project over and over. Finally, I decided to take a damage and went to take a seat on my the front porch.

As I finally started out to lighten up and search around, I discovered a massive chicken—probably a crow, however I wasn't sure—sitting at the very tip of the high-quality limb of a tree within the course of the street, more than 50 yards away. It turned into a breezy day, so the tree have grow to be swaying lightly, grade by grade in gusts. It befell to me that regardless of the truth that the chicken end up fairly big, it sat lightly at the very skinny branch, which simply need to have broken.

Not simplest that, but it remained unruffled on the dipping and swaying branch. The chicken appeared as although it modified into surfing the wind on the tree limb! Suddenly, the message end up smooth. I went again indoors, shifted gears, and cushty greater into the go together with the glide of the work. When I stopped seeking to push, matters went a first-rate deal extra smoothly.

Message acquired.

In maximum instances, the ones allies appear to us whilst wanted, to speak a few aspect of importance within the second. However, that isn't always continuously the case. Remember my earlier example with Dragonfly. Some years inside the past, Dragonfly appeared to me time and again over a duration of numerous months. As a good deal as I attempted to recognize what it turn out to be trying to tell me, not something grow to be easy.

In the give up, however, it showed up as I changed into popularity with a hard and speedy of humans. It hovered continually above one man or woman till I found out that it grow to be stating to me that I needed to be aware about that individual. He sooner or later have become an important individual in my life for a time and helped me to exchange the path of my art work. Once I "were given it," Dragonfly flew away and has not appeared so closely due to the fact that.

Though their appearances are typically unpredictable, once they show up and you're seeking out them, that they're Messengers is unmistakeable. These allies variety more than Journey Guides and really Totems.

One morning I heard the uncommon sound of Woodpecker in the distance. As I went through the day, recalling the sound once in a while, I found out that the crucial element to the sports sports of the day have become rhythm. As prolonged as I remained with the rhythm of the sports, the entirety fell into location. Yet, as soon as I fell out of rhythm, matters have turn out to be extra hard.

Just for amusing and to analyze extra about Messenger allies, bear in mind this morning workout. Before you start your day, probably earlier than you get in your automobile to energy to paintings, take five mins to take a seat down on your porch or to your backyard and just watch what is going on round you. Pay attention to the interest and find out something that catches your interest.

When you discover it, keep in mind it to be a Messenger speaking a few facts about your day. Crow browsing the wind on his tree limb board. Woodpecker knocking away at the trunk of a tree. Squirrel playing chase on the fence. Whatever it's far, take into account it every sometimes all through your day. That is a outstanding way to carry the affect and idea of Spirit without delay into your regular life.

Of route, now not all Messengers need to be animals. In the shamanic worldview, everything is alive. One each day messenger for me become Road Crew. I found that day emerge as all about deconstruction and reconstruction. Knowing that stored me a superb deal of frustration.

Shadow Animals

Eventually, everyone who practices the shamanic journey will encounter a Shadow Animal. They are sometimes frightening and threatening, yet generally intimidating. They are the beings from which you would likely maintain your distance until you're organized to stumble upon them.

The Shadow Animal is a exquisite sized presence within the Spirit international. It often gives itself as a frightening, maximum horrifying Being. They may be fireside-breathing dragons, trolls, darkish demons. They take on the face of whatever feeds your fear.

Sometimes it's miles an animal which you is probably afraid of for your normal existence, even though that isn't always a rule. People might be fearful of Spider in normal activities, but no longer in journeys, or vice versa. What is maximum essential is the manner you sense about the animal in the journey, and how it responds to you.

Shadow Animals are not similar to what's known as Shadow in Jungian psychology. It isn't always the more horrific detail of your psyche or those elements of yourself which you may select to stay hidden within the dark. It is as an opportunity a example, an archetype of Power.

In fact, Shadow Animals are allies in cover. They guard what regularly seems to be the exquisite Power that you have at your disposal. The undertaking is, "Are you prepared to absorb this Power? Are you ready to triumph over your worry and face the You that you may be?"

And from time to time, what they shield isn't clearly your hidden or undiscovered power.

Spider appeared in the course of one person's adventure. Although he generally emerge as no longer scared of spiders in everyday existence, a few element approximately this one have become very scary. Appropriately, he avoided any encounters with Spider for a long time. Eventually, despite the fact that, it have become vital for him to head on a Shadow Journey to right now have interaction Spider.

He started out, as he typically did, in his Journey Center, collecting his braveness and remedy. He referred to as his guardians to be with him, but they did now not come. It come to be clean that this become a adventure that he needed to move on on my own.

When he modified into organized, he ventured out of his safe Journey Center within the route of the dense, historical woods in which he knew Spider is probably located. Entering the woods, he determined himself at the mouth of a dark cave in which Spider lived. Of direction, it became protected with antique webbing. He paused, questioning what to do next.

Then Spider seemed in the entrance of the cave and moved closer to him.

He stood his ground and known as out. "I understand who you are," he shouted. "You are Spider and I am scared of you. But I will no longer run away this time. I am equipped for you. What do you have got to show me? What is the present which you are guarding for me?"

Spider seemed to endure in mind the query for a 2nd, then pulled out her fangs and exceeded them to him. He everyday the offers with a few wonder, then discovered himself worried that she must now not use them to devour or protect herself.

With that, Spider snatched him up and commenced out to wind him along side her silky internet. She spun him spherical, wrapping him tighter and tighter until he discovered himself no longer capable of delivery. She had cocooned him simply. Surprisingly, despite the fact that, he was no longer afraid. Instead, he modified into reminded of himself as a little one. He remembered how steady and nurtured he felt to be firmly swaddled as an toddler.

His dating with Spider took a large turn. Rather than being the fierce predator that had so significantly involved him, she have end up a nurturing presence as an opportunity. He visited her typically in next journeys, and he or she may also on occasion swaddle him in her internet at the same time as he needed some extra care. Once, he observed himself in her nest surrounded with the aid of her many infants, and it became a completely extraordinary enjoy.

The key factor to hold in thoughts about Shadow Animals is that they keep a gift, the character of which you need to earn. In many cases, you will be given presents with the useful resource of the usage of beings in your trips. Some of them are intended to transport returned with you to normal reality—to be bridged into your existence—at the same time as it's miles exceptional to go away others within the Spirit World. Mostly, these gadgets are given freely.

However, the present of Shadow Animals is robust enough that you may locate which you want to do something—or grow to be some factor—in order for it to be supplied. You want to earn it.

Related to this is the reality that there are places for your journey enjoy wherein you may no longer be allowed to move until you are prepared. Sometimes there are humans or beings which you want to approach or to realize, however they stay out of achieve, far away, otherwise you might be not able to pay hobby or understand what they will be announcing.

In those conditions, as with Shadow Animals, you would possibly find it useful to invite questions so that you can be geared up for the stumble upon. These three important questions can take you a long way in lots of adventure memories:

What do I need to realize?

What do I want to do?

Who do I want to be?

Once you examine enough about the journey and yourself, and function sufficient revel in taking walks with Shadow Animals, you may discover that they emerge as your most valued and effective allies.

Chapter 6: Spirit Animals – What Are They?

These two names are often connected plenty they end up interchangeable however they will be particular if using the proper context. Spirit animals are deemed to be the animals that could guide us or act as protectors. They may be connected to both traditional and western understandings of shamanic practices.

They will interest on a strong affiliation with someone and plenty of shamanic rituals will encompass one or distinctive spirit animals if they'll be relevant to the individual in question.

Power Animals

This tag takes topics one step similarly in which it's far the spirit of the animal that chooses the person. A person can experience one of these strong connection in each characteristics and individual that they sense drawn to a particular animal and feel that synchronicity is capability and need to be allowed to seem.

The Four Animal Guides

Just as we understand the 4 seasons, 4 colors of man, and four sacred pointers we recognize that there are also four simple kinds with regards to animal publications. It is inappropriate how an animal spirit enters our lives. It is probably through a symbolic occasion or within goals and symptoms.

The four guides are the Messenger Guide, Shadow Guide, Life Guide and Journey Guide. These can appear themselves through animal totems. Learning the versions in these four totems will assist you realize the manner you want to react and study from the revel in want to a spirit animal come into your existence. All four publications are effective.

LIFE GUIDE

Animal spirit courses are regularly related to us through animal totems. Do you do not forget having a favourite animal as a baby? Did your dad and mom buy you a fluffy animal from the zoo shop? The love and affection you may endure in mind having for your toy for all of the ones years is an indication of understand and acts as a lifelong animal totem.

Another example is if you ever hold in mind searching a specific animal for hours? You might also find you may't take your eyes of it and find yourself reading its every bypass. This is a sign of the way animal spirit courses art work. Sometimes the ones observations can come returned to you as meanings and signs and symptoms in goals.

MESSAGE GUIDE

A message animal totem is probably to preserve a sturdy message that shouldn't be ignored. This have to be seemed as a wakeup name and feel like a slap within the face.

It ought to certainly be a great and uncommon experience and might seem in short internal in all likelihood two months. Sometimes these messages may also additionally additionally appear to tell you not to do some thing or bypass someplace as though it were an instantaneous warning of horrible correct fortune earlier.

JOURNEY GUIDE

A adventure animal totem is indicative of a certain term. There isn't always any time restriction and frequently the equal animal totem will seem on your life again and again once more. Sometimes shorter durations of time might also additionally comprise one or more animals but, in assessment to the message totem performing very direct and sensible to supply its message, the animal journey totem can be extra focused on reappearance as even though to manual you or lead you.

It is not unusual for journey animal totems to slip inner and from your lifestyles at various moments.

SHADOW GUIDE

Shadow animal totems are incredibly exciting and want to in no way be left out. This is because of the fact they are sent to check us so we're succesful to overcome a fantastic private mission. At first they may appear scary and similar to a predator for your trail.

Just as in nature the religious international additionally has predators and prey however shadow animal totems aren't actually there as predators but to make us conquer our fears and act. If there may be some problem you fear that you cover from again and again then the shadow animal totem also can moreover go to to reveal you the way to rise up to these fears.

FINDING THE CONNECTION TO YOUR SPIRIT ANIMAL

Many humans surprise how they'll ever locate their spirit animal. The key may be to be open to make a reference to you spirit animal in preference to blindly going to are seeking out it out. Look for messages that could try to find out you.

You have to constantly perform a touch studies on animal habitats and possibly have a look at their lifestyles patterns inside the natural habitat. It will be very exciting to appearance how they stay to tell the story and what features they display off to get through from each day.

See thru their eyes the sector and surroundings they live in and notice from nature's aspect of view how the animal usa of the usa connects together thru the food chain to procreation and bodily cognizance of habitat.

These observations might be primarily based surely on this advanced understanding of nature and a way to take a look at nature's messages. The Indians had an first-rate deeper expertise of these messages. They proved that the medicine contained in the records of flowers and nature additionally linked everything together together with the spirit animals.

Understanding and accepting messages added from the spirit global might be used to open up all channels of the spirit international and connect with similarly records as even though the medicine modified into the important issue or life blood to all information. Other beings and spirits may be aligned collectively through the key function of medication and nature's legal guidelines.

It is consequently important to observe the paintings of communique along with your spirit manual. This might be based totally totally totally on honor and recognize and the more you can supply importance for your spirit animal the greater it will reply to you.

A spirit manual will now not with out hassle come to a person how can not pay interest or feel matters inside or enjoy nature all around them. These people may go their entire lives no longer data what they're lacking.

Let your spirit animal find you

It is critical to take into account that the animal will regularly select out the individual. The character can not consequently trade the spirit manual however simplest accumulate it and paintings in harmony with it to avoid complications in life. Individuals that aren't open to this concept will no longer be positioned. They can also strive hard. You might also see a selected animal normally at the identical time as unexpected. You may additionally moreover see ordinary animal behavior.

The exquisite manner to check in your spirit animal is to start your journey with an open mind and heart and exercise more meditation. Try and don't forget your day desires or desires in some unspecified time in the future of deep sleep. Focus on feeling the relationship.

Where can I see my spirit animal?

Here are some thoughts to be more open in your spirit animal.

• Look all round you at nature. Be observant and try to understand everything you word. Pay near interest to all of the animals you spot of their herbal surroundings and test their behavior.

• Be attentive at the same time as you notice a few issue in nature you've in no manner seen earlier than. Look at how animals act and be aware if this sends you a message in any manner.

• Look out for repeated encounters with any animals you are inquisitive about. Take below consideration this will be in physical or symbolic form.

• Study some animal behavior statistics. Learn from them.

• Meditate if you want to connecting with your spirit animal. Let them in.

• Be specially attuned to any dreams supplying animals.

• Use shamanic drumming and track at the same time as you meditate.

Use meditation to discover your spirit animal

Meditation is commonly the terrific way to discover a reference to your spirit animal. This may be for any form of interesting in that you refrain from physical sports and are allowing your mind to open and journey. Any hazard to offer your self with a certainly one of a type state of thoughts will help extensively as you'll be open to intuitive thoughts and spirituality.

How does your spirit animal seem on your desires?

Animals will frequently seem in desires so attempt to endure in mind a repeat incidence of an animal or one you have got got in no manner enjoy earlier than. They can be attempting to steer your dreams to guide you. Pay close to hobby to any messages your specific dream elements.

Some regular examples of animals in dreams, spirit or now not, are as follows.

• A lifestyles event or every other person is influencing the dreamer's life

• The spirit animal desires to come to be a guide for the dreamer

• Some feeling by way of way of way of the dreamer have no longer but been stated absolutely

• One problem of the dreamer is presently tough to control

- The dreamer goes primary instinctual emotions

Once finding your spirit animal what comes subsequent?

So in case you think you have diagnosed a connection in your spirit animal what have to you presently do? Here are some of the standard techniques to address your new thrilling situation:

Try and analyze as an lousy lot as you could about your spirit animal. Try to take a look at it in its bodily and natural shape. Use media or a few element to get a actual enjoy of this animal. Try to expect it.

As quick as viable list all of the attributes and traits of the animal you trust you studied also can now be your spirit animal. Try and do that as brief as possible as this allows discover the actual due to this in advance than you take time to do any thinking:

- Do any of those dispositions seem in relation to your questioning and feeling?

- The trends of the animal and what it represents want to have some connection memories on your existence.

- If your animal should talk to you, what do you located it'd say?

How Do you understand which spirit animal is proper for you?

First of all, it isn't always lots a query of which animal this is most vital however which one office work the nearest and maximum powerful reference to you. Here are maximum of the questions to ponder at the same time as considering the chance of which animal with a purpose to have most in common on the facet of your thoughts.

Chapter 7: Tips On How To Find Your Spirit Animal

• Your spirit animal can be a wolf, undergo, lion, cheetah, owl, giraffe or maybe a butterfly. These animals make us experience the earth or get tuned to it. Most importantly makes us make the direct selections in lifestyles. In many ideals of the severa human beings of the earth, the spirit animal is the only that chooses you in preference to you choosing them. In this situation it a matter fate that makes us have our animal spirit.

• Spending a whole lot of some time with nature is one of the techniques that makes us towards our animal spirits. The earth has a whole lot of creatures that sometimes are positioned there to educate us some topics that we do not recognise. Some humans are lucky to have a pet or as an alternative search for them and regard them as their super creatures. Some count on the pets are their animal spirit. The reality may be accurate or maybe wrong. People who have pets may be given a few credit score due to the fact they're capable of spend some time with the animals in evaluation to specific folks who spend nearly 90% in their time with different people. By having pets or generally making the natural international a bigger a part of you makes you within the course of your animal spirit.

• It is useful now not going out to look for your animal spirit but rather be open to take a look at and feature a look at more approximately all the non-human creatures. If you live in upcountry or a forested region you then without a doubt definately are much more likely to interact with nature. People who live within the towns or regions far from the individual can favor to go to a park. During the technique of analyzing nature you must make certain that you take away all of the distractions and attention at the surroundings. Try and be aware a bee landing on a flower and all of the sports activities it does with it or even birds flying spherical you. But if you are a completely busy man or woman and time is certainly a beneficial resource to you bird opt for some other manner. For instance open your property windows and concentrate to the wind as they blow. This is what may want to likely soothe you in preference to paying attention to music.

• Animals have consciousness and intelligence and you can take a step higher and begin reading their intelligence. This will carry you in the course of them. You can also be able to recollect them in another manner and begin seeing crucial matters in them. You may also be able to check their habitats and be familiar with them. It is thought that animals have a totally particular manner of talking with every extraordinary of their type. As you observe them you will probably additionally be capable of observe their method of conversation and get surprised with them. It is crucial to recognise that animals have their private varieties of intelligence. They are similar to that of humans but in a unique strategies. When you're capable of understand this and study their intelligence then it's less complicated to find out your animal spirit. If you aren't in a role then it's miles going to be tough for you. Imagine birds can excursion for a very lengthy distance and acquire their places with out the use of maps. For example in Africa, flamingos are appeared to excursion from one lake to every different during their mating and hatching seasons. For example from lake Nakuru in Kenya to lake Natron in Tanzania. This may be very exciting prevalence. Another sudden and almost unrealistic prevalence is that of the migration of the wild beasts from one difficulty of a river to every one of a kind on the equal time of the 12 months every year.

• Don't always anticipate that animals will specific themselves as people at the identical time as we term them as smart. It is important to recognize them for who they're due to the fact they are perfect of their very very own making.

www.ingramcontent.com/pod-product-compliance
Lightning Source LLC
Chambersburg PA
CBHW070554010526
44118CB00012B/1314